TOP 100

Cross Stitch Motifs

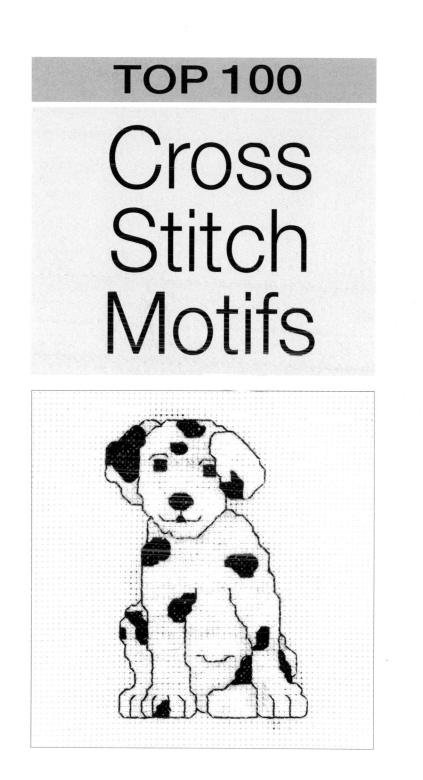

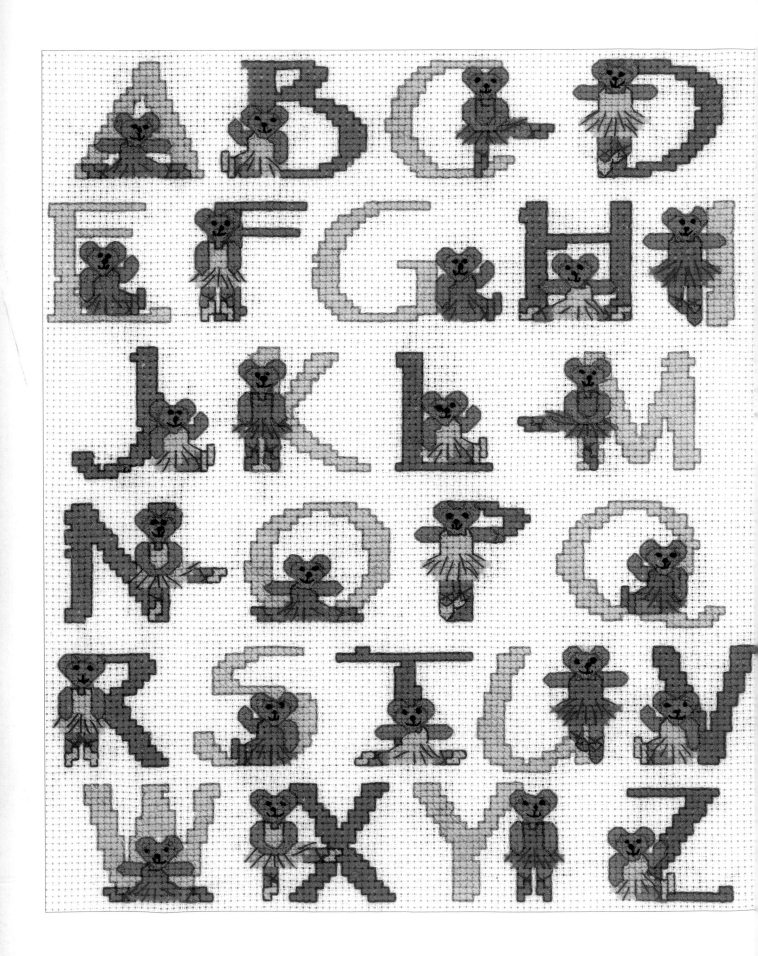

TOP 100

Cross Stitch Motifs

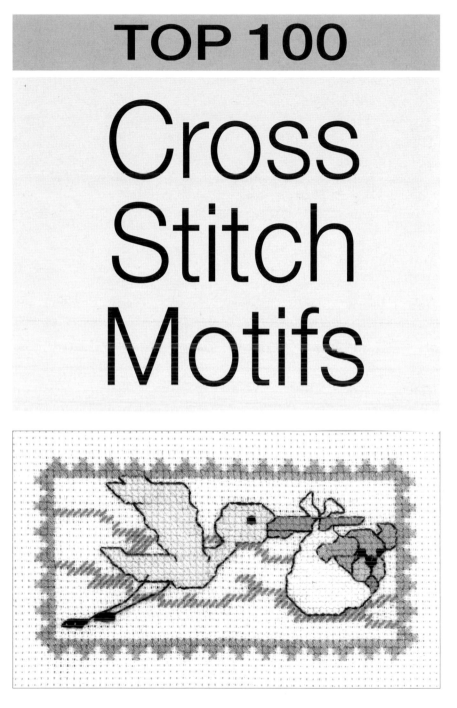

Michaela Learner

NEW
HOLLAND

ACKNOWLEDGMENTS

Many thanks go to Cara Ackerman and Evelyn Baggett at DMC (UK)
for supplying the threads and fabric for the projects in this book.

Most sincere thanks goes to my team of stitchers,
Rachael Moore, Angela Ottewell, Judy Davies, Janet Bell, Beryl Harries,
Jane Chamberlain, Jacky Kendrew.

Finally special thanks to Stephanie D'Este for stitching around the
clock to help me meet my deadlines!

First published in 2007 by New Holland Publishers (UK) Ltd
London | Cape Town | Sydney | Auckland
www.newhollandpublishers.com

Garfield House, 86-88 Edgware Road, London W2 2EA
80 McKenzie Street, Cape Town 8001, South Africa
Unit 1, 66 Gibbes Street, Chatswood, NSW 2067, Australia
218 Lake Road, Northcote, Auckland, New Zealand

10 9 8 7 6 5 4 3 2 1

ISBN 978 1 84537 678 9

Editor: Lara Maiklem
Editorial Direction: Rosemary Wilkinson
Production: Hema Gohil
Design: Maggie Aldred
Photographs: Shona Wood
Illustrations: Stephen Dew

Reproduction by Pica Digital PTE Ltd, Singapore
Printed and bound in Malaysia by
Times Offset (M) Sdn Bhd

Contents

Introduction

Over the last 15 years, working as a professional stitcher and designer, I've become aware that certain styles and sizes of motif are requested more often than others. Using this knowledge, I've gathered together a collection of motifs that represent the top 100 most requested designs.

Most of the motifs in this book can be stitched in just an evening or two, with the largest of the designs only taking around four evenings – depending on how many spare hours you have to stitch in. The motifs featured here can be recreated exactly as they are or used as a jumping off point for your own imagination.

Whether you choose to stitch a single design onto a card or a whole collection onto a sampler, for example, it's totally up to you. I've included some suggestions for using each motif, but remember, they are just suggestions so let your imagination guide you and never talk yourself out of anything – if you want to stitch a tiny teddy onto the front of a g-string, just do it! In fact, one of the advantages of small motifs is the scope they give you to play around with them a bit without having to invest too much time.

The samples in this book have been stitched onto 14-count Aida, with the

exception of the preformed bands in the border section that are a standard 16-count. Feel free to vary the final effect by changing the fabric count (just remember the count number is the number of stitches per inch of fabric) and background shade. You can also change the thread shades to suit your individual requirements – if you want to stitch a rose onto your pillow but your bedroom colour is lilac, just substitute shades of lilac for the red tones in the design.

Never allow yourself to become too bogged down by supposed "rules". If you want to start off with a knot then do it; if you don't like a shade, change it. The best thing you can do to improve your stitching is to practise; you're guaranteed to get better with each piece you stitch.

Finally, the most important thing to remember is that this is your hobby, so enjoy your stitching.

Techniques

Materials

If you are choosing to take up cross stitch as a new hobby there are some basic items you will need. As well as fabric and thread, you will need needles, scissors, a frame or hoop and a lamp. These are all described in detail below.

Fabric

This is definitely not an area you can skimp on. Spend as much as you can afford on a good-quality fabric, as this will give consistent, firm support to your stitching. Fourteen-count Aida fabric has been used for all the samples in this book, except for the ready-made bands in the section on borders (see pages 72–83).

The count number refers to the number of cross stitches per inch – the higher the number, the smaller the stitches, and the more stitches there are per inch. Which count you choose is determined by the size of your final project and by personal preference, but for most general stitching 14- or 16-count is fine.

When you are storing fabric it is best to keep it rolled up. Folding the fabric results in stubborn creases that can be almost impossible to remove, even when ironing the fabric wet. Finally, always iron your fabric before stitching. Don't assume that a crease will press out later, you need to find out whether or not it will budge *before* you spend precious time stitching!

Thread

This is another area that you should not skimp on. Buy good-quality threads – you will find them consistent in thickness, strength and colour. Unlike cheaper threads, they will also be colourfast. Believe me, it can be soul destroying to produce a lovely piece of stitching, only to have it ruined when the colours run the first time it is washed.

The standard thread for cross stitching is stranded cotton (embroidery floss). DMC threads, with six strands and sold in 8 m (26 ft) skeins, have been used for all the projects in this book. You can also get speciality stranded threads – I have used DMC Light Effects, DMC Pearlescent, DMC Rayon and DMC Colour Variations to jazz up some of the designs.

Needles

I find economical, blunt-ended tapestry needles just as good as the more expensive gold-plated ones, as I tend to only use my needles for three or four projects before discarding them. New needles slip easily through the fabric and are lovely to use. As a needle ages, sweat and oil from your fingers can cause the surface to roughen and it then becomes less likely to glide easily through your fabric. With older needles the eyes can also become worn and develop little burrs that can shred the stranded embroidery thread.

Use a size 20 or 22 tapestry needle for projects stitched on 14-count. A size 22, 24 or 26 needle should be fine for 16- and 18-count projects. That said, my personal preference is for as fine a needle as can take the thread. It is always a good idea to practise on some scrap fabric, see which needle best suits your project and stitching style, then go with that. Try buying an assorted pack of needles until you develop a liking for a certain size.

Scissors

A variety of embroidery scissors are available to suit all budgets. As a general rule though, the more you spend, the longer they will last. The scissors themselves are small, 8–10 cm (3–4 in) long, and come with vicious points for snipping off close to your stitching and for unpicking.

It is worth either buying or making a scissor case to hang around your neck. I'm forever losing my scissors when I'm stitching and have the scars to prove the number of times I've sat on them – I've even skewered my foot! If nothing else, I suggest using a long bootlace looped through one of the handles and slipped over your head – believe me, it'll be a lot less painful in the long run.

Another thing to bear in mind if you intend to stitch while travelling by air is that most airlines will not allow scissors on board. You can get around this with thread trimmers, which look like little discs and are accepted by most airlines. They are also relatively inexpensive so if they do get confiscated on your way through check-in, it's not the end of the world.

Frame or hoop

I prefer to use a floor-standing frame, with what looks like two large wooden screw threads the full length of either side. It means I can keep my hands free while stitching projects that range in size from the width of the frame and any length (just roll the excess fabric around the frame), to as small as 2.5 cm (1 in) square. This is invaluable when it comes to stitching preformed Aida bands (see page 14, Special Techniques).

Personally, I'm not keen on embroidery hoops because of the damage they can cause the fabric, which can be almost impossible to iron out. The only time I use one is to hold scrap fabrics for practising techniques before using them on my frame projects. (You can build up an interesting scrapbook of techniques by keeping your practice pieces.)

If you do prefer to use a hoop make sure you get in the habit of removing the fabric from it whenever you have finished stitching for the day – this will at least minimize the crush damage caused. Also, take care when repositioning it so that you don't damage the areas you have already stitched. Use a larger hoop if possible.

Floor-standing frames can be a bit pricey, but they are well worth the investment if you intend to do a lot of stitching or a large project. Holding onto a frame or hoop can cause horrible hand cramps, so you will find that using a floor-standing frame will allow you to keep stitching for longer. If you can't afford a new floor stand try finding a second hand one. Certainly, much of my arsenal of stands has been obtained from Internet auctions at a fraction of the cost.

Lamp

While not a necessity, a good lamp can be invaluable when working in the evening. I use a basic angle-poise lamp bought from a DIY store with a standard 60-watt daylight bulb. By using a daylight bulb I find I avoid misidentifying colours and I'm able to stitch for long hours without any eye strain or headaches. You'll find there are many daylight products on the market to suit all requirements and pockets.

The Basics

The guideline instructions given here are simply that, guidelines. They are based on techniques I have personally developed over the last 15 years as a professional stitcher. If you have a way of doing things that suits you better then please go ahead and do it. Nothing is written in stone, it's your hobby and it's supposed to be fun so don't get bogged down with rules – I hate rules!

Preparing your fabric

First of all, contrary to common myth, size does matter. When you are setting up, allow for the size of your chosen design plus *at least* 10 cm (4 in), more if possible. This will give you a minimum margin of 5 cm (2 in) around the edges of your stitching that will allow for mounting your piece or simply trimming away any distortion or damage that has been caused to your work by the frame or hoop.

Having established the size, you next need to find the center of the fabric. Do this by folding the fabric in half and then half again. The point where these folds intersect will be the center. Tack (baste) in two short intersecting lines of thread to mark it.

A good habit to get into is to count out from this center line and to mark the edges where the stitching will finish with a couple of tacking (basting) stitches. This will ensure your starting position is correct and that the fabric is large enough. It will also help guide you when mounting the fabric ready for stitching. Give your fabric a final press before mounting it.

Once the work has been mounted on a frame and you have started stitching at the center point, the tacking (basting) stitches will have served their purpose. I would suggest removing them as soon as you feel happy to do so as they can start to get in the way of your work and get caught up in your cross stitching.

Mounting fabric on a frame or in a hoop

There are several types of frame on the market. I like to use one that involves stitching the Aida fabric to a strong webbing, which I do with some uneven cross or half cross stitching (see illustration 1).

As I have said before, I don't recommend using an embroidery hoop (see page 9), but if you do choose to use one I suggest you sandwich a layer of tissue paper or tear-away stabilizer between your Aida and the hoop. Then just tear away the center to expose the Aida and stitch.

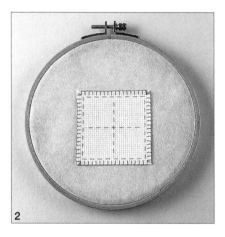

If you are working with a very small piece of Aida you may want to tack (baste) it to a piece of tear-away stabilizer and then mount that into a large hoop (see illustration 2). This means the fabric isn't touched, and therefore can't be damaged, by the hoop. Also, there is nothing more fiddly than trying to weave in thread ends when you are using a hoop that is barely wider than the length of your sewing needle.

Threading your needle

Cut a length of embroidery thread from the skein, approximately 50 cm (20 in)

long, or the length from your fingers holding the thread almost to your underarm. Individually withdraw the required number of threads from this length – usually two for cross stitch and one for backstitching – and thread them together in your needle. Alternatively, cut a 1 m (40 in) length of thread, withdraw one thread and fold it in half, then thread the needle with the loop furthest away from it.

Don't be tempted to withdraw more than one thread at a time from your cut length of embroidery thread. Firstly, they will knot and tangle as you try to remove them, and secondly your stitches won't lie evenly if the threads haven't be separated and recombined.

Following a chart

Start stitching from the center and work outwards. Technically it is good practice to begin stitching with pale shades and finish with the darker ones. This stops dark fibers, deposited by the stitching action, from contaminating white and pale shades. If you do have to start with dark areas, try dabbing over your work with some sticky tape to remove any deposits of dark fibers before starting the paler stitching. Also bear in mind that if you trail dark thread across the back of a pale area it will "ghost" through your work, so try and avoid this.

Sometimes beginning with pale shades isn't practical so look carefully at the chart to see which symbols or shades jump out at you and start with these instead. This will make it easier for you to identify your place when your eyes are scanning between the chart and your stitching. Try positioning

some small self-adhesive sticky notes on your chart to mark where you are working – this is particularly helpful if you are working on a larger project.

Stitches

The methods featured here are simply the way I cross stitch. If you have a preferred technique and are happy with your results then I suggest you stick with it.

Starting and finishing

There are three main ways to secure the thread when you start stitching. It's useful to familiarize yourself with all of them as each has its place in helping you produce neat even stitching.

Waste knot

Thread the needle with two separate 50 cm (20 in) threads and knot one end. Work out where you want to start stitching then count five or six blocks horizontally to the left and pass the needle from the front to the back, leaving a knot on the surface. Bring the needle up at your starting point and, when you begin cross stitching, make sure the first couple of stitches go over the trailing thread on the reverse side, thus securing it in place, then trim away the knot. This method is great when you first start doing cross stitch.

Loop stitch

Cut a length approximately 1 m (40 in) from the skein and withdraw one thread. Fold it in half and thread your needle with the loop furthest from it. Pass the needle from the back to the front of the fabric in the exact place that you want to stitch. Now, pass it back through at the next point in the stitch, making sure the needle goes through the loop – this will secure the thread in place. This method is by far my favourite and the one I use the most. It minimizes the number of cut ends on the back of your work and prevents stray fibers from complicating things on the back of your work.

Threading under

This method works for both starting and finishing off. Working on the reverse of the work simply pass the needle under a couple of stitches, preferably of the same shade, to secure the thread in place.

Cross stitch worked in rows

Stitch with the needle at 90° to the fabric using a "stabbing" motion. This is the best way of stitching as it minimizes distortion to the Aida fabric and it is easier to get a good, even tension on the stitches. The single most important thing with cross stitch is to ensure that your stitches all run in the same direction.

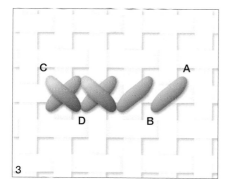

Bring your needle up at A and pass back down at B, repeat until you have as many stitches as you need in a single row. Then bring the needle up at C and pass it down at D, taking care

not to pull too tightly. Repeat this back across the row of stitches to your starting point (see illustration 3).

It may seem a bit of a fiddle at first, but a good habit to get into is a method of stitching called railroading, or tramlining – this produces neater, more even stitches. On the second half of the stitch, as you are passing the needle back through the fabric, take it between the two threads of stranded cotton (embroidery floss) that are already in place. Do it often enough and it will become second nature – you will be amazed at the effect this can have on

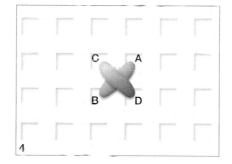

your stitching.

Cross stitch worked individually

Sometimes only one stitch of a certain shade is needed. To do this bring the needle up at A, down at B, up at C and down at D (see illustration 4). Take special care that the stitches all run in the same direction.

If more stitches are to be formed try not to trail thread too far across the back. Where possible trail the thread horizontally or vertically with the expectation of anchoring it in place when stitching with a different shade.

Half cross stitch

This is simply one "leg" of a cross stitch. You can work this in either direction –

just look at the project and decide which way you think will look best. You may wish to experiment on a piece of scrap fabric to help you determine which direction you prefer, or you may want to use both directions and form a chevron. Just go with what looks best.

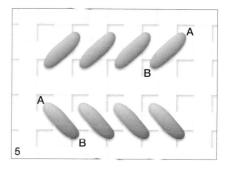

Bring the needle up at A and down at B (see illustration 5).

Partial stitches

Partial stitches are represented on a chart with a small symbol in the corner indicating the stitch direction. Which stitch or combination of stitches you choose is up to you (see illustration 6). My personal favourite is to use three-quarter stitches in pairs when two symbols appear in one square on a chart. This way you can keep the stitches lying in the same direction and you don't end up with sparse patches. If you choose to do a quarter stitch and a three-quarter stitch just work out which part of the stitch represents the background and that will be your quarter stitch. One thing to note is that if a project contains a lot of partial

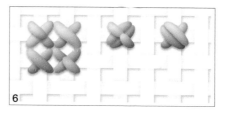

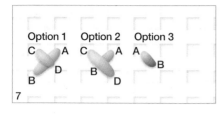

stitches you may wish to switch to a needle that is a size smaller. There are various ways of working these partial stitches, as shown in illustration 7.

Option 1 A three-quarter stitch worked against the direction of full cross stitches. Bring the needle up at A, down at B, up at C and down at D. Stitch into the center of the Aida block by holding the needle at 90° to the fabric and gently wiggling it while producing light downward pressure. You'll find that it will just slip between the fabric fibers.

Option 2 A three-quarter stitch worked in the same direction as the full cross stitches. Bring the needle up at A, down at B, up at C and down at D.

Option 3 A quarter stitch that can be worked from any corner. Bring the needle up at A and down at B.

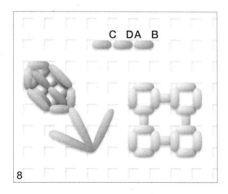

Backstitch and straight stitch

Bring the needle up at A, down at B, up at C, down at D, and so on for a classic backstitch (see illustration 8). Sometimes it is necessary to stitch over more than one thread, but the basic method is still the same. When an individual backstitch is indicated it is called a straight stitch, but it is worked in just the same way.

A pattern formed using just backstitch is called blackwork. It doesn't have to be in black thread and can be lovely worked in colour over a background of cross stitch – see the underskirt of the princess on page 107 for an example of this.

French knots

This is a stitch that is often feared by novices, but it really isn't that difficult – just spend 20 minutes practising on a piece of waste fabric and you'll soon get the hang of it. If you absolutely hate French knots, however, then substitute small seed beads instead – it's your hobby after all and you are supposed to enjoy it!

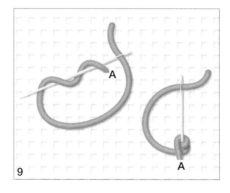

Bring the needle up at A in the position you want the knot. Keeping the trailing thread taut, twist the point of the needle around the thread twice. Pass the needle back down at A and slowly pull the thread through. Stop as soon as the trailing thread has disappeared and a knot has been formed (see illustration 9) – if you pull too hard the knot will disappear through the hole in the Aida.

Finishing your work

It is important to take a bit of care to finish a project off properly as this can really be the making of a stitched piece.

Washing

If you are very careful when you are stitching then washing the completed work may be unnecessary. However, if the final piece has been on a frame for a while, or if it has just had a bit of a hard life, then it will need some freshening up.

So here I'm in a quandary. As a professional I should tell you to gently hand wash the piece in mild detergent. However, three-quarters of the projects featured in this book were simply thrown in the washing machine on a 40° wash with standard non-biological washing powder, and they all survived. So take your choice, but remember the second method is the more risky one!

Pressing

Firstly, put a thick, fluffy towel on your ironing board – try giving it 10 minutes in a tumble dryer before you do. Set the iron to a medium heat, unless the work has metallic thread, when it should be set to cool or the thread will melt – another lesson I learnt the hard way!

Iron your piece when it is damp. Press it on the reverse side until it is virtually dry – the towel will help the stitches stand out instead of flattening them. If your fabric has become distorted, give it an initial light press on the reverse and then pin it out while it is still damp to square up the sides. Leave it to dry naturally.

Storing

If you need to store your work before framing it, either keep it flat or roll it in a towel or around a cardboard tube. Never fold your work across the stitched area as you will never get rid of the creases.

Mounting a greeting card

Cards come in a variety of types so here are two methods that should work for most of them.

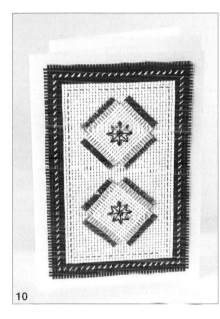

10

Bi-fold cards

These are the everyday cards you would recognize in a shop – one piece of cardboard folded in half with no aperture (see illustration 10). They are useful if you are trying to mount a non-standard size design, as you can make them from your own card stock if necessary. How about folding your own envelopes to match the card? Have a quick search on the Internet and you will find lots of websites to show you how to do this.

Trim the fabric so it's the same size as the card, or slightly smaller.

Pull away some threads at the edge of the Aida to create a small fringe then either glue or, better still, use double-sided sticky tape to attach it straight onto the front of the card.

11

Tri-fold cards

These cards are traditionally sold for mounting cross stitch designs. They have three sections, with an aperture in the middle one (see illustration 11).

Trim the fabric so it will fit inside the card. Attach double-sided sticky tape to the card around the aperture edge, position it over the stitching, making sure it's lined up, and press down.

At this stage you can lightly pad the reverse with a piece of felt or wadding (batting) cut slightly smaller than the aperture. I'm not a fan of doing this, especially if your card is going through the post, as it can cause the card to crease at its thinnest point by the aperture.

To finish up, again use double-sided tape to stick the card over the back of the stitching.

Mounting for framing

Before a piece of cross stitch is framed, it is best to mount it onto a piece of cardboard. You'll need a suitable mount board cut to size and some crochet cotton to lace it to the board.

Place the stitching on the front of the mount board. When you are happy with its position push some pins down each side into the board and double-check the position is correct.

Trim away the excess fabric, leaving approximately 5 cm (2 in) all around. Fold two opposite sides to the back of the mount board. Starting with a knot, use crochet cotton in an under-and-overstitch motion to lace the opposing edges of fabric together, while the pins keep everything in position on the board. Before you secure the thread, lightly adjust the laced threads by gently pulling to ensure a nice even tension.

Fold over the remaining edges of the fabric and repeat the process. Lastly, remove the pins.

Special techniques

When you are ready to progress to the next level with your cross stitching, the following techniques should allow you far more creative freedom with your projects.

Using waste canvas

Waste canvas – a fabric that is loosely held together with starchy glue, which dissolves when dampened – is used when you want to work cross stitch onto a non-evenweave fabric. It acts as a removable temporary grid for the cross stitches (see illustration 12). Not all designs are suitable for waste canvas. Try to choose solid designs and avoid areas of just backstitch, which tend not to look very good when the waste canvas is removed.

Tack (baste) center vertical and horizontal lines onto the waste canvas itself and then tack the whole piece to whatever you want the cross stitched motif to end up on. Take great care to position your waste canvas in the correct place and make sure that it's level.

When stitching your crosses make sure you don't inadvertently pierce any of the fibers of the waste canvas, as this can make it very difficult to remove them afterwards. The type of needle you should use is determined by the fabric you are stitching onto, but some sort of crewel needle is usually best. Try buying an assorted pack so you have a choice.

There are two ways of stitching on waste canvas. Option 1 is the generally recognized way of doing it, which I hate, and option 2 is how I actually do it (see illustration 12).

Option 1 Stitch the crosses into the large holes. I find this a bit hit and miss as great care has to be taken to make

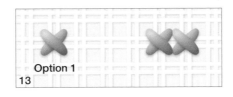

Option 1
13

sure the crosses are touching or you end up with gaps when you have finished (see illustration 13).

Option 2 Stitch your crosses into the small intersecting holes. This may seem a bit tricky at first, but it doesn't take long to get the hang of it and the result is far neater (see illustration 14).

Option 2
14

Illustration 12 also shows this second option as described above.

After stitching with your chosen method, remove all the tacking (basting) threads and dampen the canvas to dissolve the glue. You will then be able to remove the canvas threads. Use a pair of tweezers to remove any that are reluctant to come out. If they still resist lightly dampen the work and try again.

The final result will be helped by a light press on the reverse side over a fluffy towel (see page 12).

Using preformed Aida bands

Preformed bands are an easy way of adding cross stitch to a variety of items – towels, bags, curtains (drapery), bedding, in fact just about anything you can think of. They are available in a number of thread counts, although the most common is 16-count, and a variety of widths to suit different projects. They are completely finished

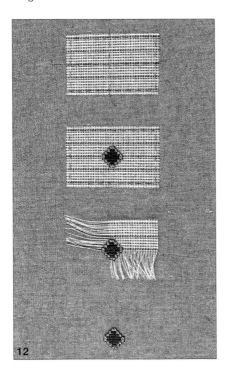

12

along the long edges so all you have to do is tuck in the ends when you are attaching the band to your project.

To stitch a band just mount it in a frame, if you're lucky enough to have one as adjustable as mine, or across an embroidery hoop. I find it easiest to start stitching in the center then work outwards, evenly and either side, until the correct length is reached.

Stitching with speciality threads
Metallic, rayon and pearlescent threads
These threads should all be tackled in the same way. To thread a needle, take one long strand and double it over. Pass the loop through the needle eye and then pass the needle back through this loop. You will end up with the thread securely attached to the needle. This makes it a lot easier to stitch with as all these special threads have a tendency to fall out of the needle eye, thus making it difficult to keep a good tension on your work. You might also want to consider changing to a larger needle than usual as this will help the thread pass through the fabric by enlarging the hole slightly.

Stitch as for stranded cotton (embroidery floss), but work slowly. If you attempt to speed up, these threads will tangle and knot. This is where floor stands become really useful as it helps to have both hands free to guide the threads as they go through the fabric.

Try a couple of practice pieces on some spare fabric before using them on a project. It's surprising how quickly you can get used to them and they give a lovely lift to a project.

Colour variations thread

There are a number of different ways of stitching with variegated thread, but I'm only going to outline three of the most popular ways. The different methods result in a different distribution of the colours, so the choice is yours. This is a thread where a few minutes spent practising will reap ample rewards.

Cut a 40 cm (16 in) length from the skein. Remove two threads, recombine and thread them onto your needle. This method of threading will give a shaded effect. Stitch whole individual stitches at a time, not rows.

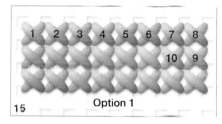

Option 1

Option 1 Start at 1, stitch a whole stitch then keep stitching in rows back and forth. This will give a striped effect (see illustration 15).

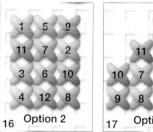

16 Option 2   17 Option 3

Option 2 Place individual stitches totally at random for a really wild pixelated effect (see illustration 16).

Option 3 Graduate stitches out from a corner point, working in an arc. This will give a shaded, tie-dye type of effect (see illustration 17). You can also work this way going from outer edges inwards.

Stitching alphabets

When stitching alphabets there is no hard and fast rule when it comes to spacing. Some alphabets work well with structured spacing, for example the large stripy alphabet on pages 30–31, while others are better with random spacing and some overlaps, for example the fairy alphabet on pages 26–27.

If you are in any doubt try drawing the outlines of the letters onto some squared paper, cut them out and fiddle around with them until you come up with something that pleases.

Another way to stitch alphabets is to try doing them "ransom note-style", using letters from each different alphabet. This can be really effective and even spacing is not a consideration.

Creating a sampler

The earliest known sampler dates back over 400 years. Modern samplers are very similar, in that they are a collection of varied motifs and borders arranged in a way that's pleasing to the eye.

There are many ways to approach designing a sampler. The easiest is to use a computer program. If you are designing by hand, however, you will need some squared paper. You may find it easiest to just sketch the outlines of motif shapes rather than copy them entirely. Either sketch the whole design in rough on one piece of squared paper or, if you find working on a large scale a bit daunting, sketch each motif outline on some 14-count squared paper (see illustration 18). Then pin these onto 14-count fabric to get an idea of placement and whether the different motif sizes work together.

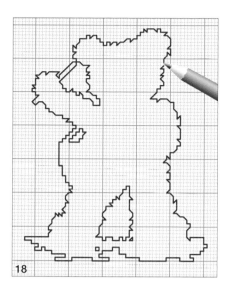

Work out the size you want the final sampler to be and add a border inside that boundary. Next, add an alphabet and some numbers, which are traditional on a sampler. Somewhere on your design you will then want to include either your name or initials and a date or year, so that in years to come your piece will become a treasured family heirloom (providing you manage to get it stitched!). Fill in the gaps with your chosen motifs. Do this either in structured rows or take a more random approach, which is more forgiving if you make a placing error when stitching – three guesses which method I favour!

A sampler can be themed, for example the motifs can all be teddies, about a new home or a new baby, or it can just be a collection of your favourite motifs. It's totally up to you – you are the designer after all so just relax and immerse yourself in the creative process and don't try to rush it. If you hit a problem go off and have a cup of coffee and come back to it with a fresh pair of eyes and a clear mind. Above all enjoy yourself!

Alphabets

Alphabets are an ideal way to quickly personalize a stitched piece. Whether you choose an individual letter or a whole alphabet they never fail to give a pleasing result.

This straightforward, lower case alphabet is a real workhorse. It is an ideal choice when work space is limited, e.g. on a card, or if you are planning on adding a lot of text, e.g. stitching a favourite poem or song. Try combining them with fancy capital letters, changing the shades used to match your project.

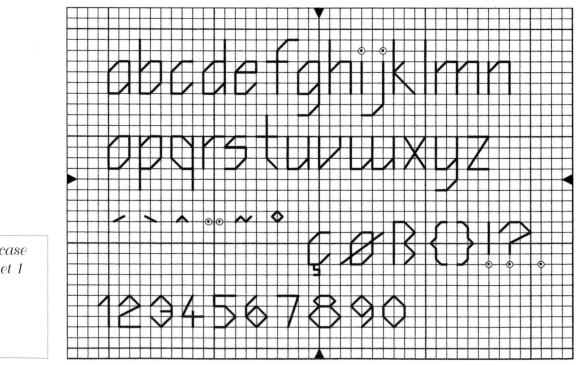

Lower case alphabet 1

— 3842
● 3842

The ultra-modern and crisp shape of this alphabet perfectly represents the 21st century. It stitches best when worked onto smaller samplers (15 cm (6 inch) square or less) and cards. It can also easily be combined with one of the lower case alphabets if more complex wording is required.

Modern alphabet

■ 3803

— 3746

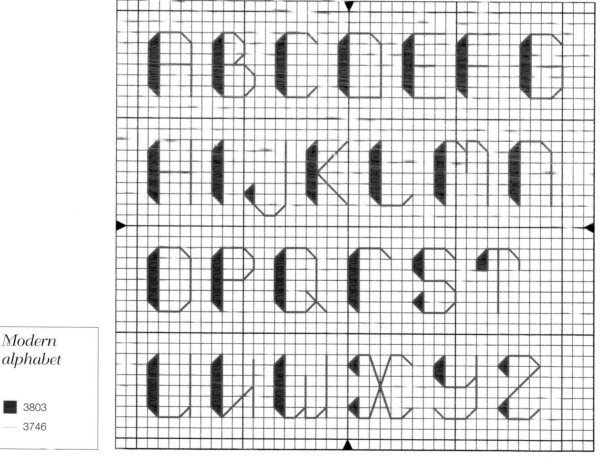

This great utility alphabet is suitable for many projects. It reminds me of the sort of letters that are used to teach children to read and write – neat and very precise. For this reason this alphabet works well when stitched onto a project for a child. Add a name to a gym bag or pencil case, or try making decorative flash cards for a child's room in a lettering style that's instantly recognizable to them.

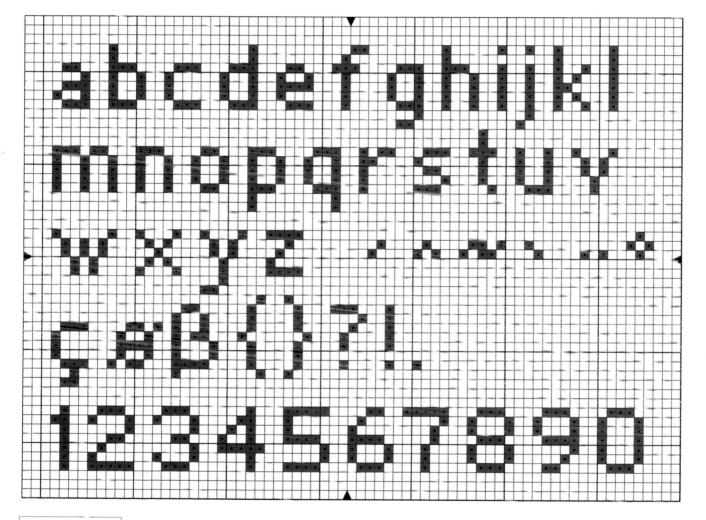

*Lower case
alphabet 2*

■ 995

These mini bears are a firm favourite with everyone I know. In fact I love them so much that they reappear in their gym kit on pages 36–37. Individual letters can be used to personalize items or to make a decorative card, alternatively try scattering the entire alphabet randomly across a baby blanket for that special little girl.

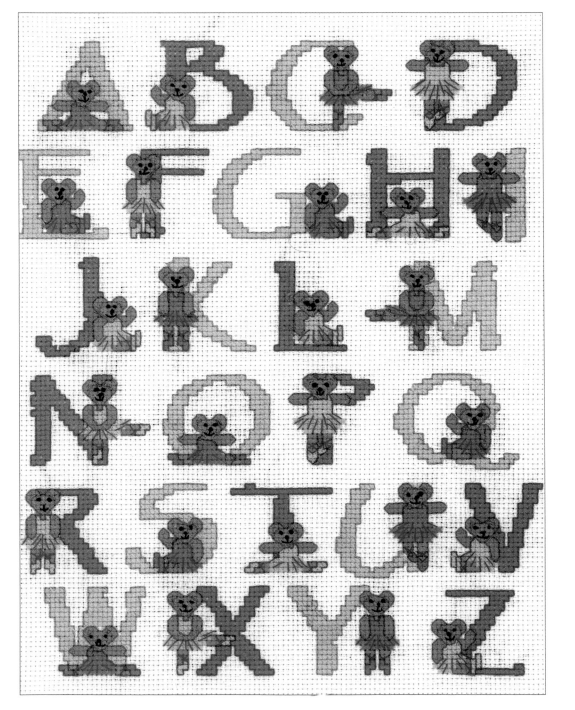

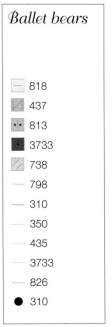

Ballet bears

⊟	818
▨	437
⦙⦙	813
▣	3733
▨	738
—	798
—	310
—	350
—	435
—	3733
—	826
●	310

Backstitching
Dresses 798, 350
Letters 3733, 826
Face 310
Body 435

French knots
Face 310

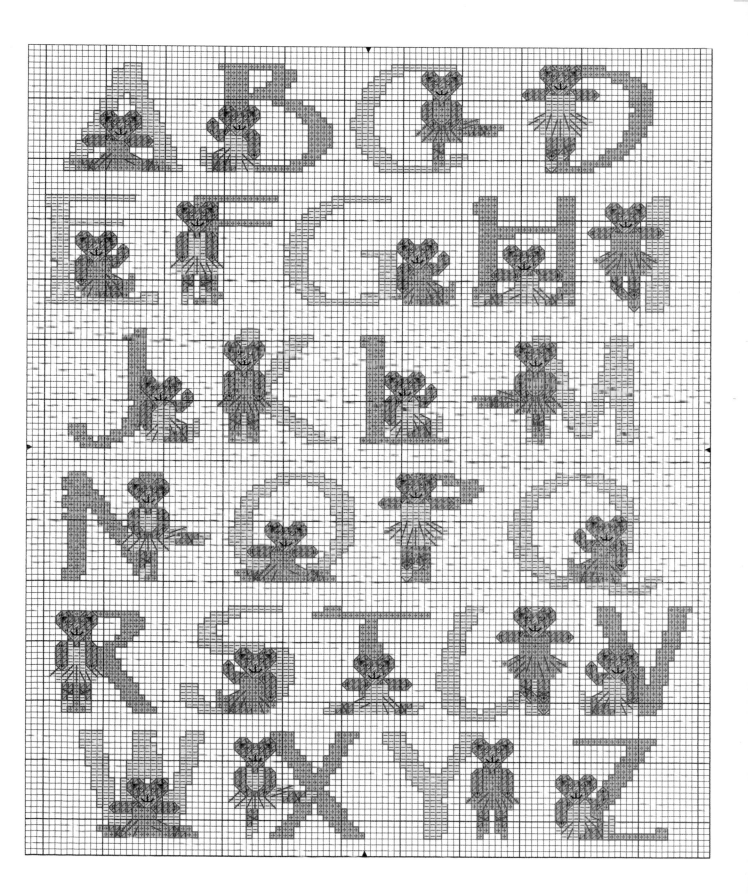

The butterflies give this subtle alphabet a real dream-like quality making it the perfect choice for decorating bedroom items. Why not use it to personalize keepsake bags or to monogram a dressing gown, or try stitching individual butterflies fluttering across a pillowcase or cushion cover.

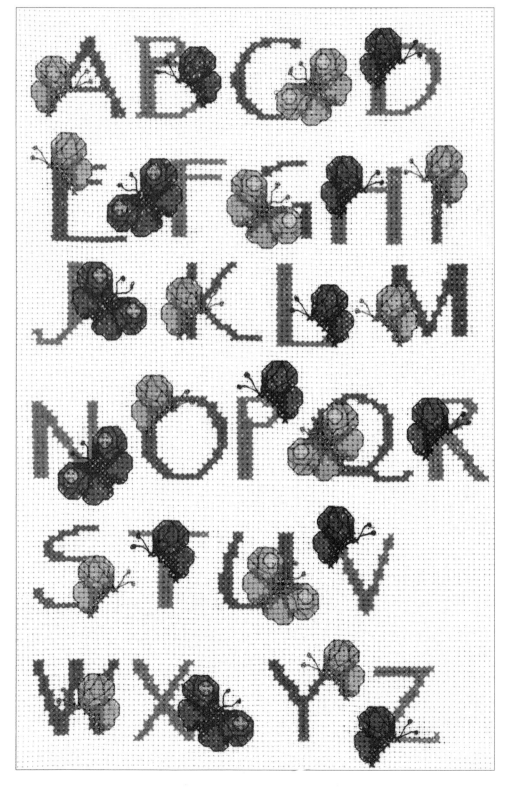

Butterflies

⠿	Pearlescent 211
⟐	209
⬡	208
•	948
↑	353
⬥	352
■	Light Effects Jewels E3837
■	Light Effects Jewels E316
—	3685
—	Light Effects Jewels E3837
—	Light Effects Jewels E316
●	Light Effects Jewels E3837
●	Light Effects Jewels E316

French knots
Purple butterfly   E3837
Peach butterfly   E316

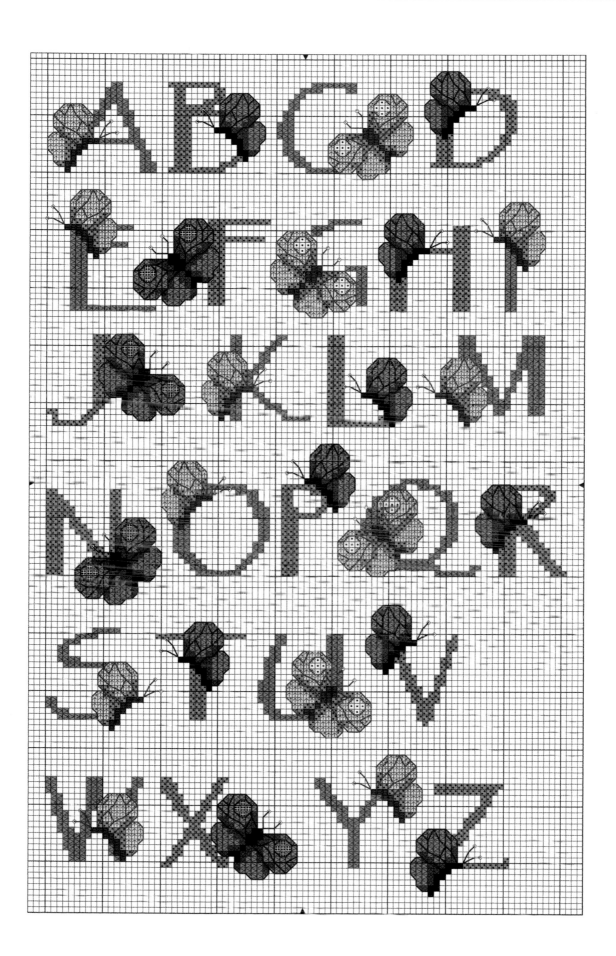

This delicate, quick to work alphabet has a lovely, gentle shaded effect and is deceptively simple to stitch as all the flowers are identical – master one and you've mastered them all. It's the perfect accompaniment to a floral sampler, or stitch the whole alphabet ready for framing, maybe adding a border of flowers to finish it off.

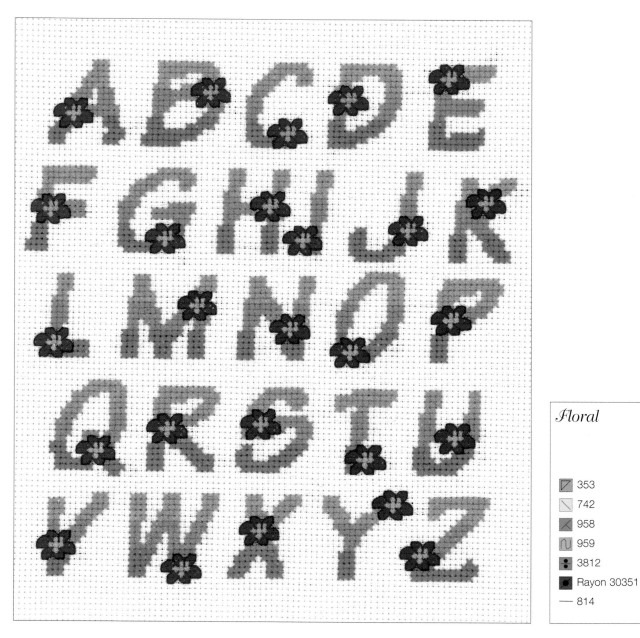

Floral

◪	353
◲	742
◪	958
◠	959
⦂	3812
◼	Rayon 30351
—	814

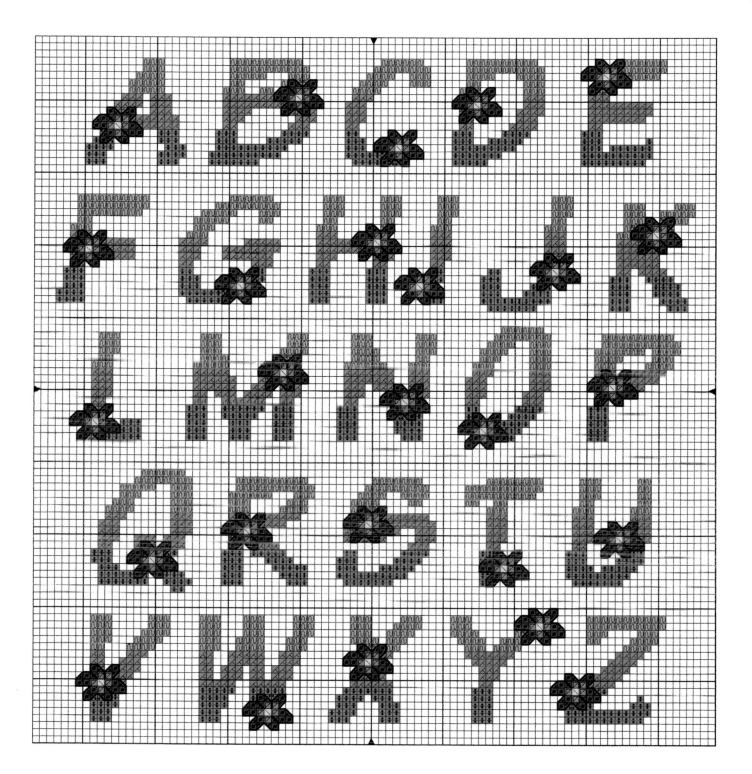

The fairies in this alphabet give it a definite touch of whimsy.
Use it as charted for a decorative picture, add it to a sampler,
or stitch random letters to liven up plain bedroom curtains
(drapery) or vertical blinds (shades). You could also stitch
single fairies onto cards or clothing – try working them on
individual patches and then appliqué onto your chosen item.

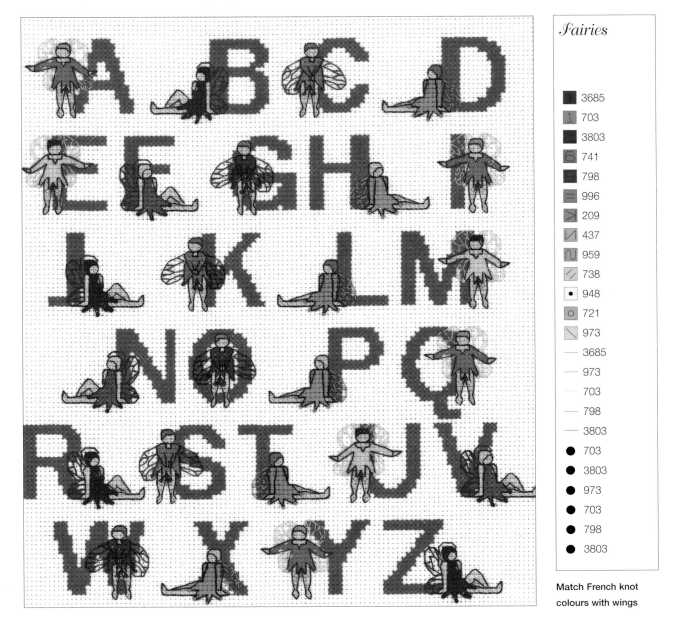

Fairies

■	3685
1	703
■	3803
6	741
■	798
▬	996
▷	209
◩	437
Ⴖ	959
⁄	738
•	948
o	721
◥	973
—	3685
—	973
—	703
—	798
—	3803
●	703
●	3803
●	973
●	703
●	798
●	3803

**Match French knot
colours with wings**

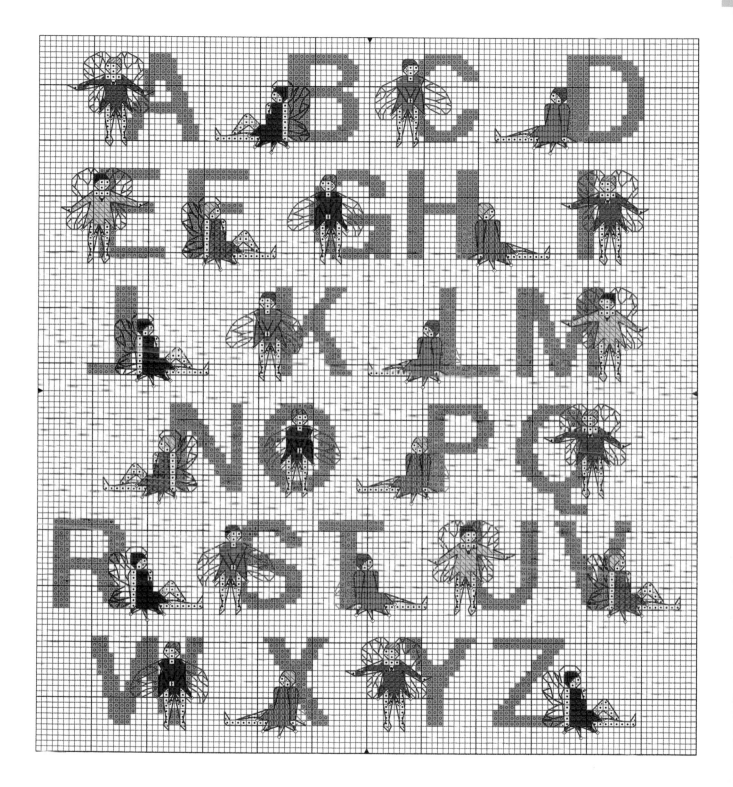

This striking, bold, geometric design is great for making a statement. Use it to stitch a child's name onto a laundry bag or use it to make bedroom door name plates. Use individual letters on patches to brighten up a pair of curtains (drapery) or a bedspread, altering the colour/colours you use to suit your room theme.

Patchwork

■ 350

— 814

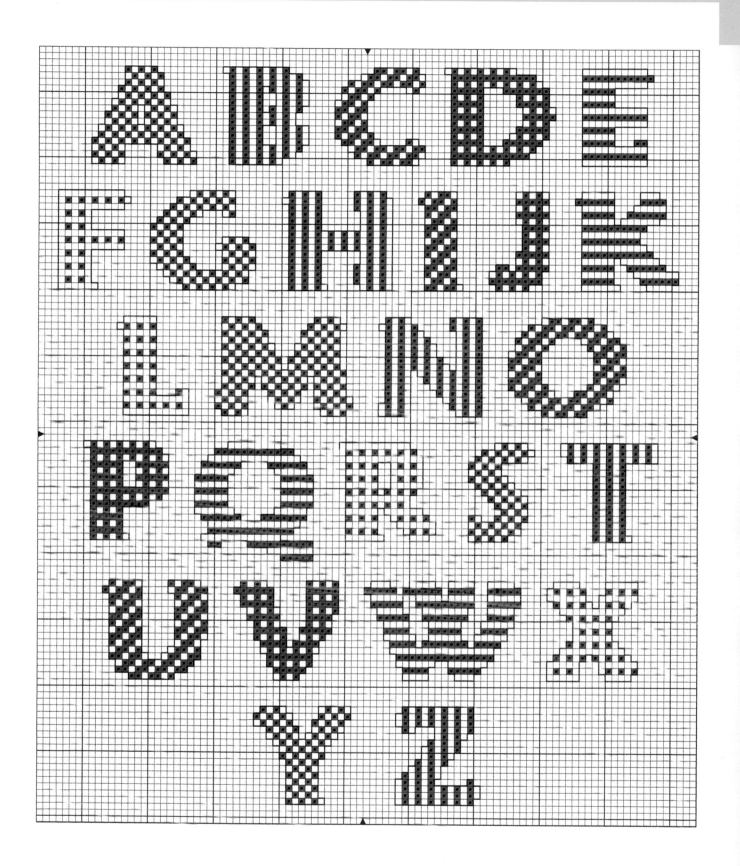

This bold alphabet is suited to large scale lettering projects, perhaps a wall banner for a special occasion (use a different shade for each letter) or personalizing a bag or rucksack. This style of lettering is also good for using up waste canvas, so try stitching individual letters onto some denim and appliqué them onto a cushion (pillow) cover.

Stripe

▦	820
•	Blanc
—	823

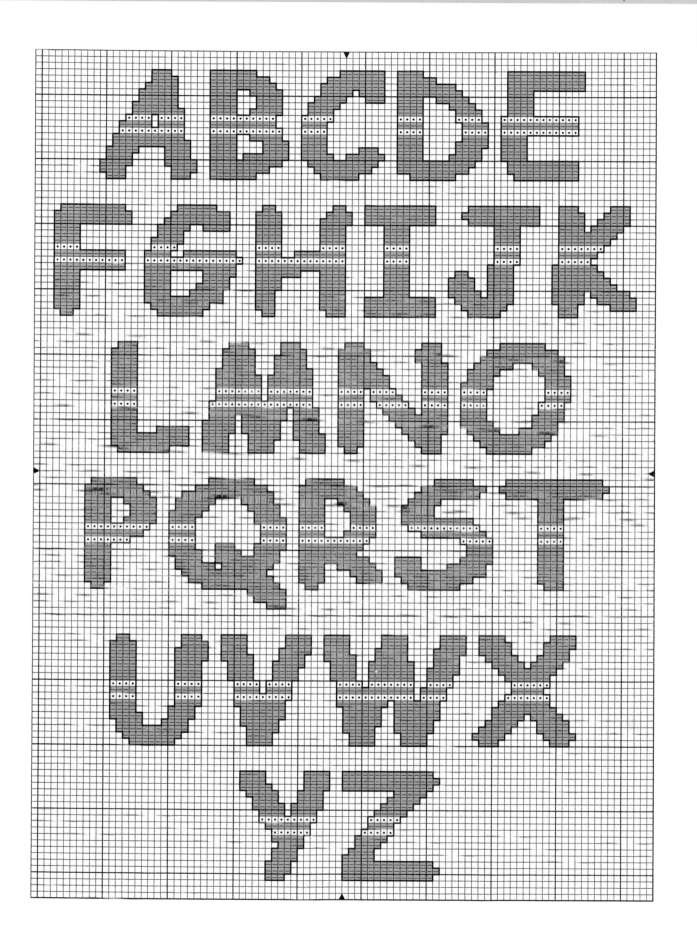

Being mid-sized, this alphabet is possibly one of the most versatile. Stitch the whole alphabet on a sampler or use the letters to add wording to a scrapbook project, combining it with one of the lower case alphabets. The individual sparkly areas can also be stitched separately and used to cheer up clothing or a festive table cloth.

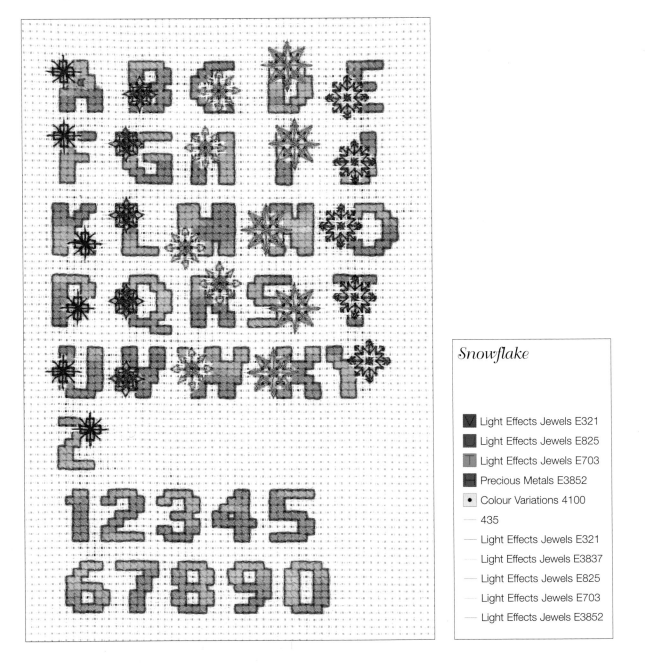

Snowflake

V	Light Effects Jewels E321
■	Light Effects Jewels E825
T	Light Effects Jewels E703
H	Precious Metals E3852
•	Colour Variations 4100
—	435
—	Light Effects Jewels E321
—	Light Effects Jewels E3837
—	Light Effects Jewels E825
—	Light Effects Jewels E703
—	Light Effects Jewels E3852

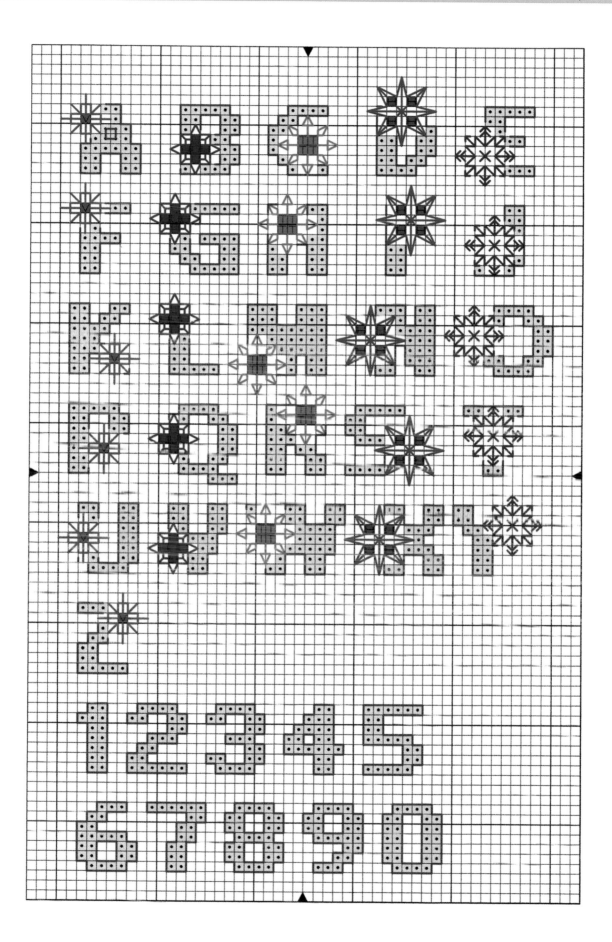

Teddies

Few can resist the adorable charm of teddy bears. They have a timeless appeal to everyone, which makes them one of the most versatile motifs available.

This nurse is a favourite for get well soon gifts and cards – who could fail to be cheered up by her welcoming arms, always ready for a comforting cuddle? Stitch her onto cards and fabric notebook covers or add her to a teddy sampler.

Nurse bear

‒	437
⊥	738
■	300
⁊	3716
◼	666
⊥	712
◉	796 half cross stitch
▼	796
•	Blanc
⊠	3024
—	300
—	796

The heart tattoo on this noisy little bruiser's arm proves he's really a softy. Stitch him up into a lovely framed picture for the little, and not so little, man in your life. If time is pressing why not just work his smiley face onto a card.

Drum bear

■	300
7	3716
♥	666
▣	3829
/	729
⊖	677
→	746
▢	743
S	743 half cross stitch
◪	703
—	300
	743

These active mini bears can inspire anyone to
go to the gym. Stitch individual bear motifs onto
patches and appliqué them on gym kit items;
alternatively work the whole design onto a
gym bag. Try changing their leotard colours
to make use of any left over threads you have.

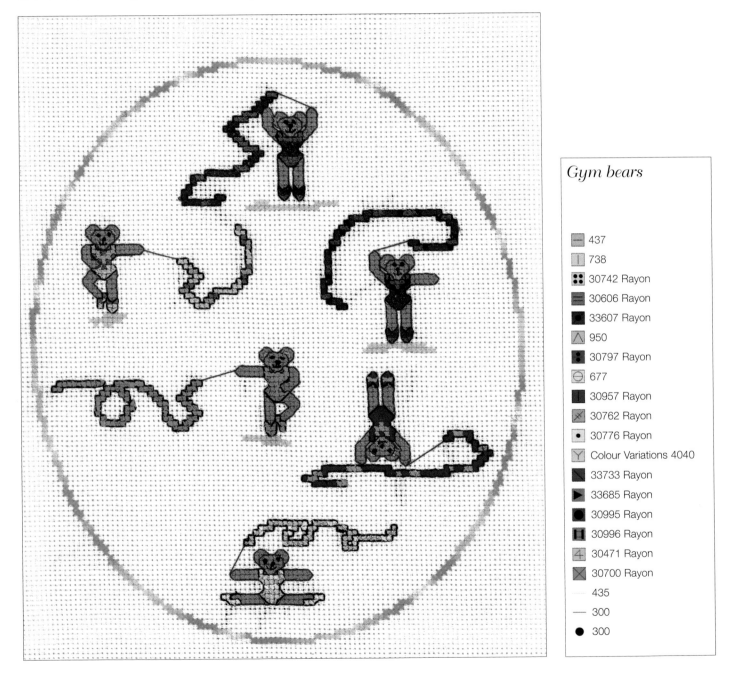

Gym bears

Symbol	Thread
⊟	437
‖	738
∷	30742 Rayon
☰	30606 Rayon
■	33607 Rayon
∧	950
▮	30797 Rayon
⊖	677
▐	30957 Rayon
⊠	30762 Rayon
•	30776 Rayon
Y	Colour Variations 4040
◣	33733 Rayon
▶	33685 Rayon
●	30995 Rayon
∐	30996 Rayon
⊿	30471 Rayon
✕	30700 Rayon
	435
—	300
●	300

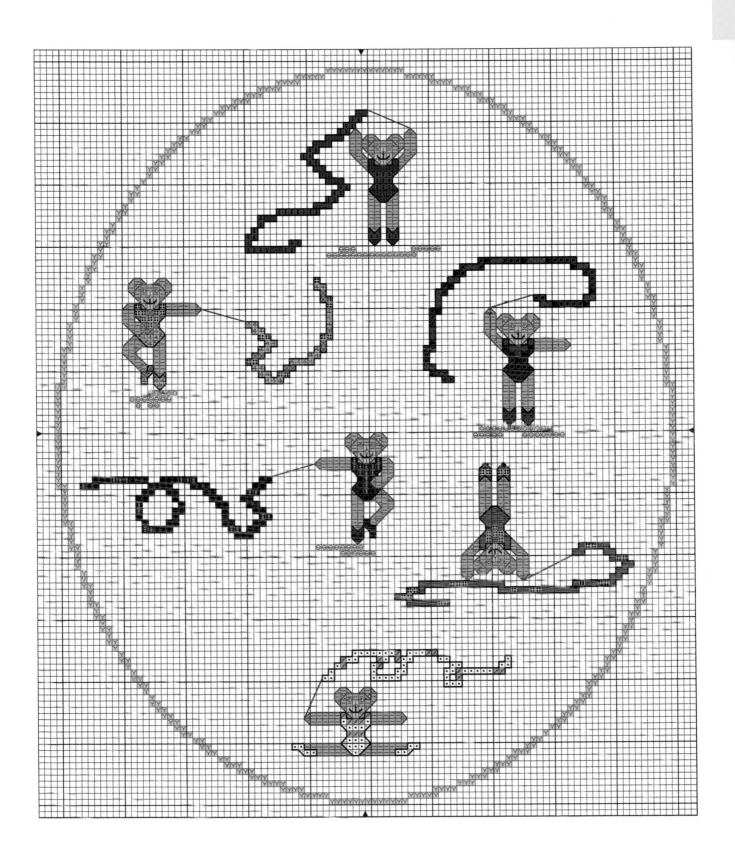

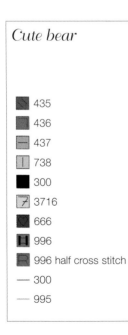

This cute and friendly bear design is one of the most versatile in this section. His small size makes him ideal as a card or use it as a design for a gift for a friend. Change the colour of his scarf and the shadow to suit your individual requirements.

Cute bear

◣	435
	436
⊟	437
Ⅰ	738
■	300
⧅	3716
■	666
Ⅱ	996
⊞	996 half cross stitch
—	300
—	995

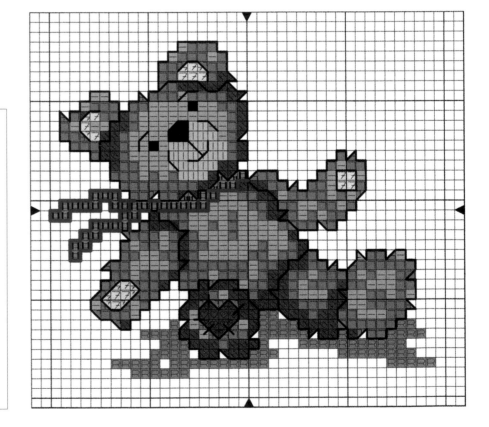

Sleeping peacefully, this dozy little bear is ideal for stitching onto baby bedding. He also looks great decorating a bib or bonnet, or work just his face and arms onto the toes of bootees. Remember to make sure all your ends are very secure for items that are likely to be laundered often.

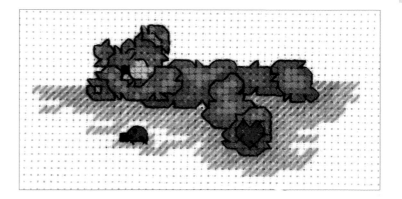

Sleepy bear

- ■ 435
- ■ 436
- ▬ 437
- 1 739
- ■ 3371
- 7 3716
- ■ 666
- 703 half cross stitch
- ✕ 701 half cross stitch
- — 3371
- ● 3371

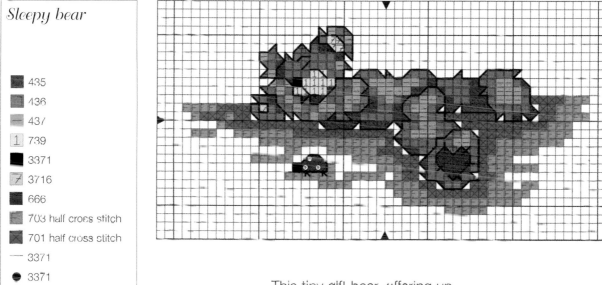

This tiny gift bear, offering up a gold ribbon wrapped parcel, is a firm favourite. Use him as a gift tag, card or stitch as a mini picture for a compact or mirror bag. Best of all, he makes a wonderful peace offering when you've put your foot in it!

Gift bear

- ■ 434
- \ 435
- ■ 436
- 1 738
- ■ 300
- 7 3716
- ■ 666
- 703 half cross stitch
- Z 703
- — 300
- — 30742 Rayon

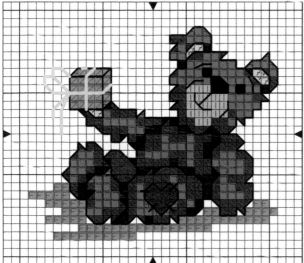

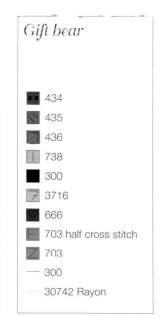

This big daddy bear motif is a stately looking fellow, with his wine red waistcoat and blue folded hanky, who would make a lovely gift for a father or grandfather. Work the whole design as a cover for a notebook, or for the more time pressed stitch just his face onto the case of an mp3 player or mobile phone.

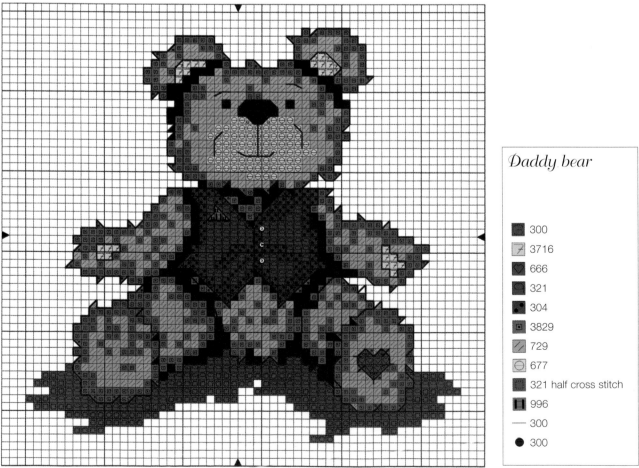

Daddy bear

■	300
⊿	3716
◥	666
▦	321
◾	304
⊡	3829
⁄	729
⊖	677
▦	321 half cross stitch
▐	996
—	300
●	300

This is just how I remember my grandmother: small, cuddly and always baking in an apron. This motif works well as a recipe book cover, just add a border of honey bees and some small lettering for a fantastic result. If a smaller project is required try stitching just the honey pot and bees.

Honey bear

▨	436
▨	300
⁊	3716
∩	209
•ı•	3820
+	3822
⊖	677
→	746
•	blanc
▢	743
▤	703 half cross stitch
⊿	703
—	300
—	3041
	743
●	300: cake mix, apron
●	3041: sleeves
●	Blanc: eyes

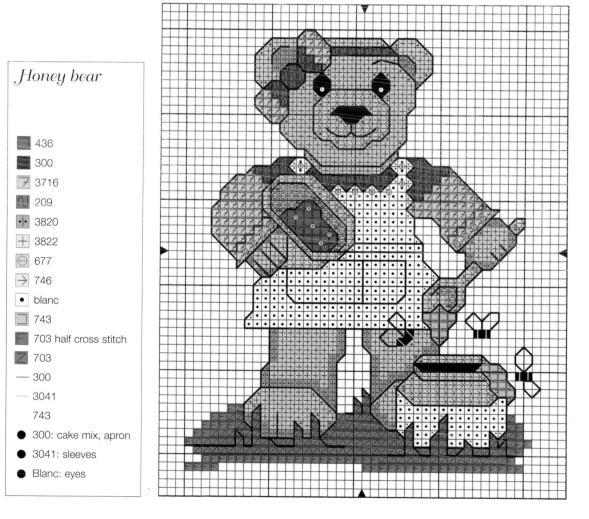

Perfect for young and old alike, this teddy bears picnic is a great project for using up oddments of thread, just change the clothing and picnic item colours to use up what you have available. The individual bears can be worked up for cards and scrapbook projects.

Picnic bears

- | 738
- 1 739
- 300
- 4 704
- 666
- 740
- 407
- 209
- 3820
- 746
- Blanc
- 826
- 743
- 603
- — 300
- — 666
- 743
- ● 300

Up, up and away with this adorable balloon bear. The fuzzy, creamy-coloured bear is ideal for stitching onto bedroom items. Work him onto curtains (drapery) or a pillow case, adding extra balloons to fill up the area. You could also stitch multiple images randomly onto a child's duvet cover.

Balloon bear

—	437
I	738
■	300
7	3716
♥	666
⊖	677
→	746
▢	743
▦	603
■	666
N	3747
—	300
—	666

Christmas

Each of these small festive motifs will only take a couple of hours of your time to stitch. This makes them ideal at such a busy time of year, when there is so much to do and so little time to get it all done in.

Stitch this cheery Santa, with his sack crammed full of gifts, as a jolly card or work him onto plastic canvas for a tree ornament. If time is really short just stitch his rosy face onto some plastic canvas and glue it onto a bi-fold card for speedy results.

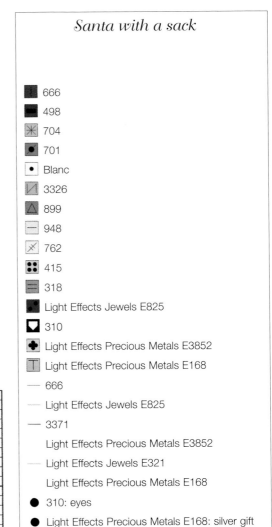

Santa with a sack

▮	666
▬	498
✳	704
⬤	701
•	Blanc
◪	3326
△	899
▬	948
✕	762
⦂⦂	415
▭	318
▪	Light Effects Jewels E825
♡	310
♣	Light Effects Precious Metals E3852
⊤	Light Effects Precious Metals E168
—	666
—	Light Effects Jewels E825
—	3371
	Light Effects Precious Metals E3852
—	Light Effects Jewels E321
	Light Effects Precious Metals E168
●	310: eyes
●	Light Effects Precious Metals E168: silver gift

This easy little Santa band stitches up very quickly. It is good for festive table linen – edge tablemats with a repeating band or stitch individual motifs onto napkin corners.

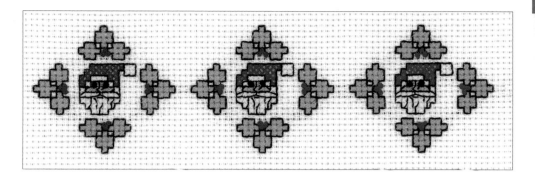

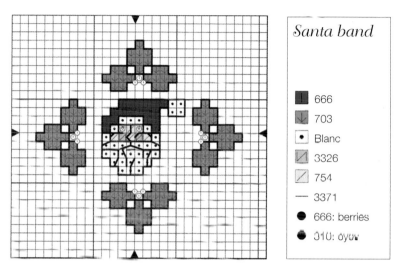

Santa band

■	666
↓	703
•	Blanc
◿	3326
◿	754
—	3371
●	666: berries
●	310: eyes

Santa in a chimney

■	666
•	Blanc
◿	3326
△	899
—	948
◿	754
✕	762
◿	796
◥	310
✚	356
◉	355
—	3371
	Light Effects Precious Metals E3852
●	Blanc: snowflakes
●	310: eyes

Stitch him onto a Christmas card and Santa's happy face and pink chubby cheeks are sure to bring a smile. If you don't want to stitch the sky try working on navy fabric instead. This design can also be used on a Christmas stocking, just add the person's name above or below.

What more could you want under the tree on Christmas morning than a lovely pile of presents? Work this as a complete picture or just stitch the bows to make speedy gift tags or napkin decorations. If you've got threads to use up, just alter the gift wrap shades to use them up.

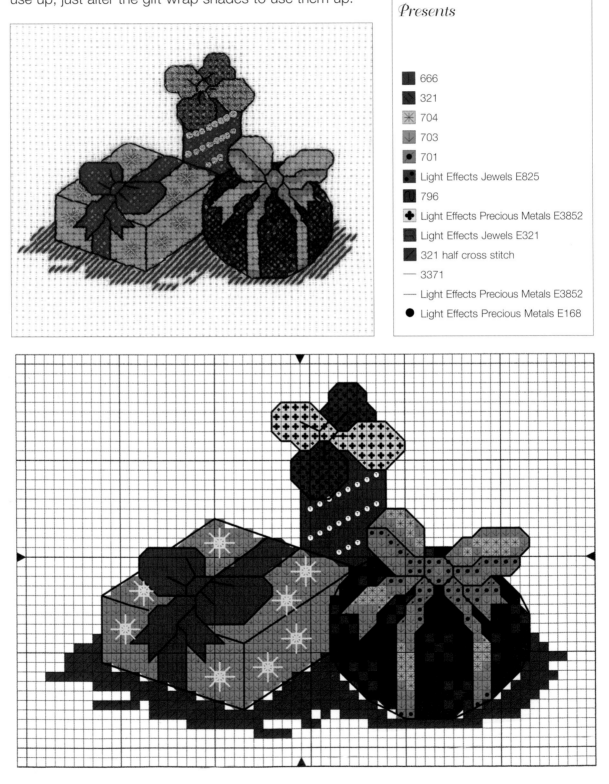

Presents

▨	666
▨	321
✳	704
↓	703
●	701
▨	Light Effects Jewels E825
▨	796
✚	Light Effects Precious Metals E3852
▨	Light Effects Jewels E321
◪	321 half cross stitch
—	3371
—	Light Effects Precious Metals E3852
●	Light Effects Precious Metals E168

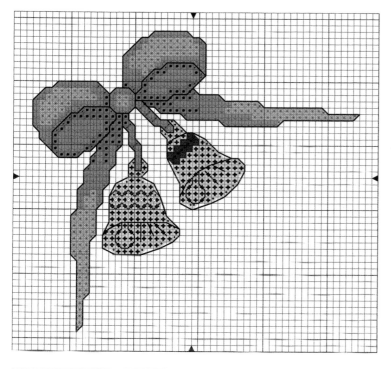

Traditional bells make this a firm festive favourite. Stitch individual motifs for decorations or cluster four motifs to make a stunning tablecloth centerpiece. Change the ribbon colours to suit your table theme and try experimenting with silver bells.

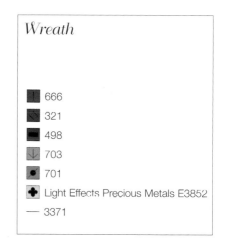

Bells

* 704
703
701
Light Effects Jewels E025
Light Effects Precious Metals E3852
Light Effects Jewels E321
— 3371
— Light Effects Jewels E321
● Light Effects Jewels E825

This timeless wreath is one of the most versatile motifs in this section. Use it for a card or tree ornament or on table linen and festive guest towels. Stitch just the bow, repeated along the edge of a pillowcase or cushion cover.

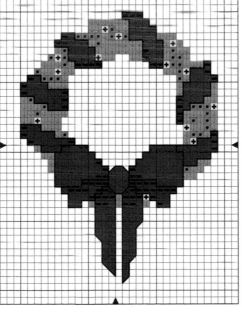

Wreath

666
321
498
703
701
Light Effects Precious Metals E3852
— 3371

This chilly snowman, with his big coal smile and carrot nose, makes a lovely Christmas card or a tree ornament when worked onto plastic canvas (just omit the partial stitches on his nose and work with whole ones instead). Try adding him to brightly coloured Christmas linens or stitch just his scarf and head for an eye-catching gift tag.

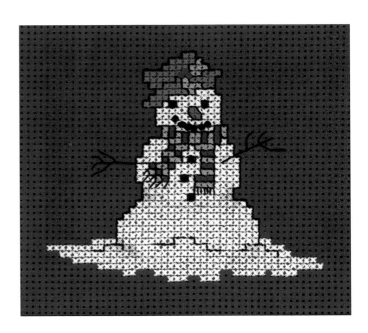

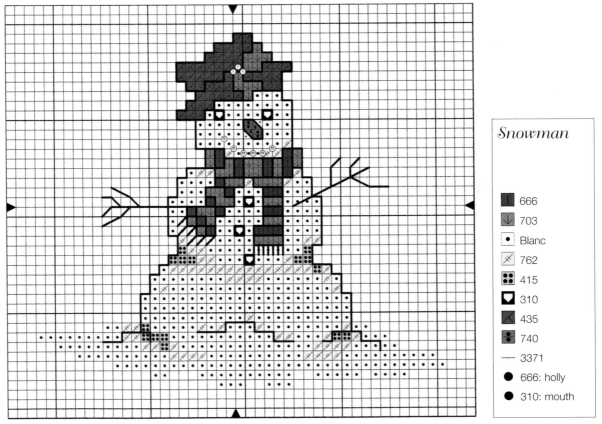

Snowman

▮	666
▼	703
•	Blanc
✗	762
⁚⁚	415
◨	310
◩	435
⁞	740
—	3371
●	666: holly
●	310: mouth

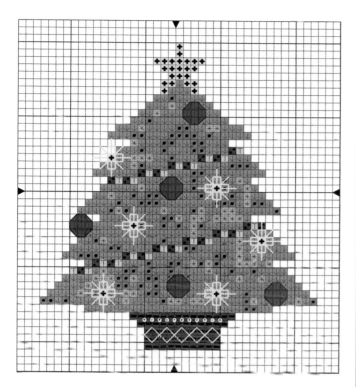

This time-honoured Christmas tree, with twinkling lights and a bright star, is an ideal festive image. Use it in scrapbooking or try combining it with the Santa band on page 45. If you don't have much time, stitch just the star for a speedy gift tag.

Christmas tree

666	
498	
704	
703	
701	
Light Effects Jewels E825	
Light Effects Precious Metals E3852	
Light Effects Precious Metals E168	
Light Effects Jewels E825	
Light Effects Precious Metals E3852	
814	
Light Effects Precious Metals E3852	

The single Christmas candle is a very tasteful design and works well on a festive sampler, card or tag. The best thing about this motif is that it can be worked in an hour – a fact that saved my neck last Christmas!

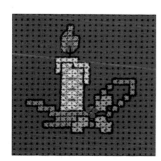

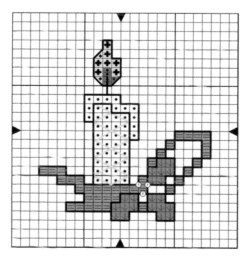

Candle

703	
Blanc	
318	
740	
Light Effects Precious Metals E3852	
3371	
Light Effects Precious Metals E3852	
666	

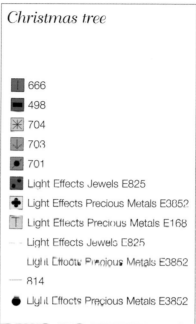

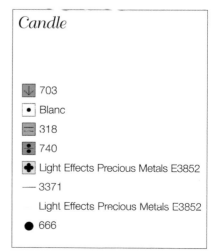

Rounding off this section is a
collection of sparkly snowflakes.
These very versatile motifs have a
number of uses – scatter them across
a Christmas table cloth or stitch them
as tree ornaments, cards, tags or on
festive stockings. Change the shades
to make use of any spare metallic
threads you have – purple and silver
make a modern alternative.

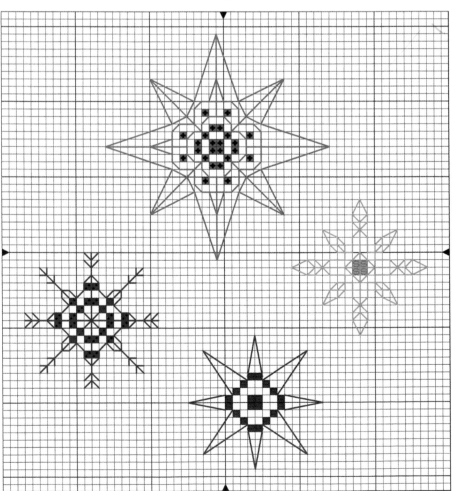

Snowflakes

■	Light Effects Jewels E825
◆	Light Effects Precious Metals E3852
■	Light Effects Jewels E321
S	Light Effects Jewels E703
—	Light Effects Jewels E825
—	Light Effects Precious Metals E3852
—	Light Effects Jewels E321
⋯	Light Effects Jewels E703

Little uns

These cheeky designs are inspired by and for the smallest members of your family. Be sure to stitch them before your bundle of joy arrives!

Baby with bottle

- • Blanc
- ▉ 601
- ▦ 799
- ▦ Colour Variations 4190
- ◯ 819
- ▬ 818
- ᴓ 3713
- — 300

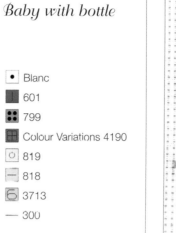

A cheeky grin and a kiss curl on the forehead makes this an adorable motif. Stitch it onto bibs and clothes, or make a great "welcome to the family" card. This motif stitches in a couple of hours so why not use it to while away those boring early hours of labour – or perhaps not!

This is a lovely memento of a baby's first tooth. Put it in his or her baby book to commemorate the landmark or use it on baby clothes. This filled design is ideal for working on waste canvas.

First tooth

- • Blanc
- ▉ 606
- ◪ 340
- Y Colour Variations 4080
- ◯ 819
- ▬ 818
- ᴓ 3713
- — 300

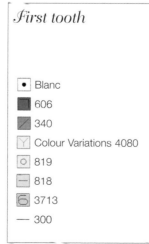

This Jack-in-a-box design really reminds me of my own childhood. It makes a cheery picture for a child's bedroom or add it to a cot set for a brighter alternative to all those pastels. Alternatively, stitch just his face and spotty tie onto fabric and appliqué it onto clothing.

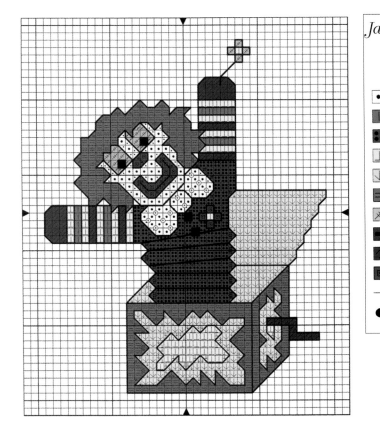

Jack-in-a-box

•	Blanc
	3608
	798
	307
↓	444
	740
✕	563
	3857
╱	3837
	666
—	3857
●	666

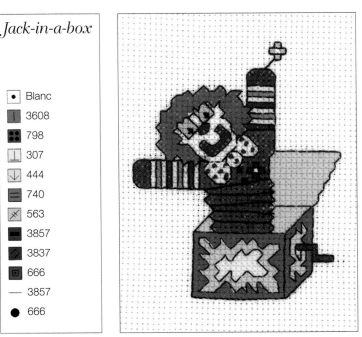

The pram in this design is given a lovely lift by stitching it in colour variations thread worked on the diagonal. Try repeating the motif for a decorative band for a cot set.

Pram

	606
6	945
╱	Colour Variations 4220
✕	563
	552
╱	973
W	563 half cross stitch
—	300
●	300

Rocking horses are often treasured favourite toys, so much so that many of us keep them into adulthood. Stitch this one as a cozy bedroom picture or as a cover for a baby book – just add a very simple border of single cross stitch in colour variations thread for the finishing touch.

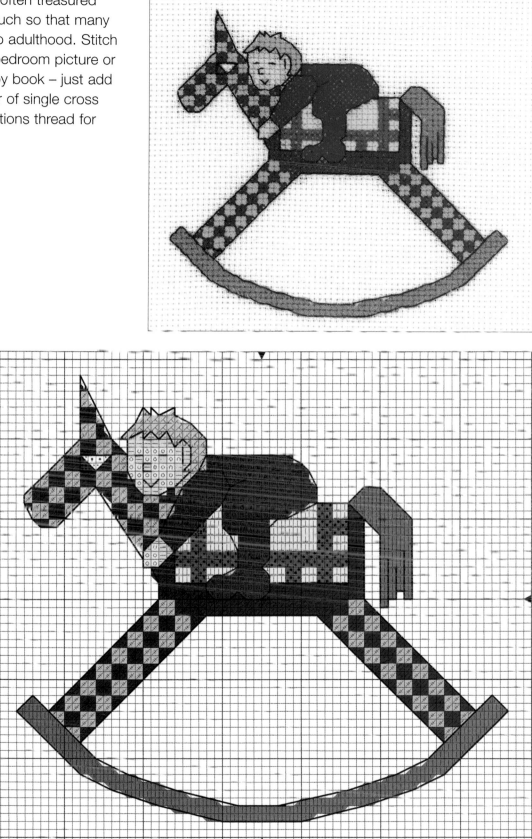

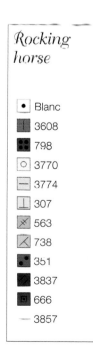

Rocking horse

•	Blanc
▨	3608
▦	798
○	3770
—	3774
⊥	307
✕	563
◹	738
•	351
◩	3837
▣	666
—	3857

This design captures an array of beautiful babies from all over the world. Stitch individual babies as spot motifs on clothing or bedding, or, for a real statement piece, work as many repeats as your nerves can cope with on 11-count using three strands cross stitch, and frame the result. The more repeats, the more jaw dropping the result.

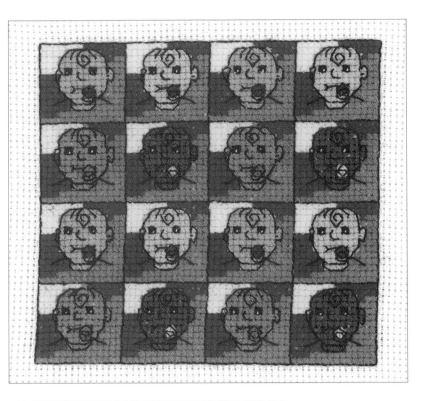

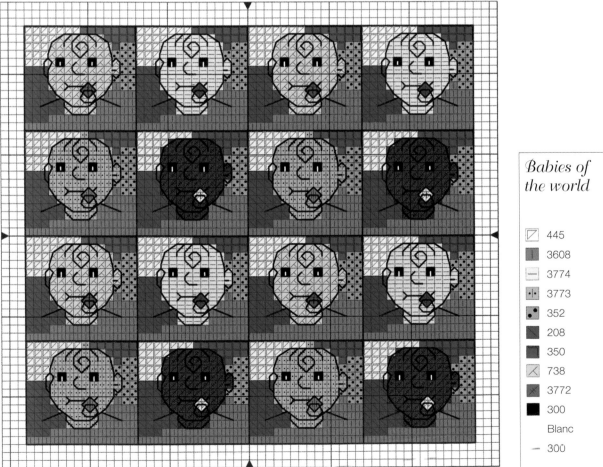

Babies of the world

▧	445
▦	3608
⊟	3774
⊡	3773
⬤	352
◼	208
◼	350
◹	738
◩	3772
◼	300
	Blanc
—	300

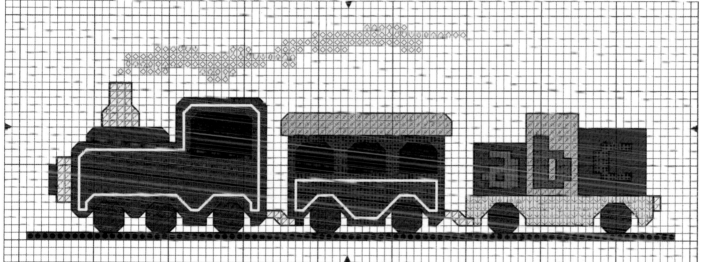

This section wouldn't be complete without a train motif. Add carriages in different shades to suit your requirements and stitch it onto curtain (drapery) borders and bedding. Alternatively, work it onto fabric and glue it onto a toy box; by adding some lettering in the same way you will end up with a unique piece of nursery furniture.

Train

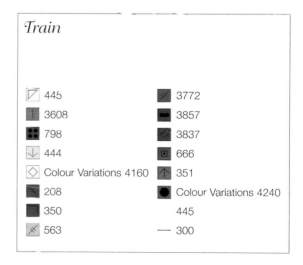

◹ 445	⊠ 3772
▯ 3608	▬ 3857
⊞ 798	◿ 3837
↓ 444	⊡ 666
◇ Colour Variations 4160	↑ 351
◣ 208	● Colour Variations 4240
▮ 350	445
⤬ 563	— 300

Is there anything lovelier than a peacefully sleeping baby? Stitch this as a framed picture or use it in a baby sampler as a feature motif. It has been designed to be gender neutral so try altering the colours to suit the baby you are stitching for.

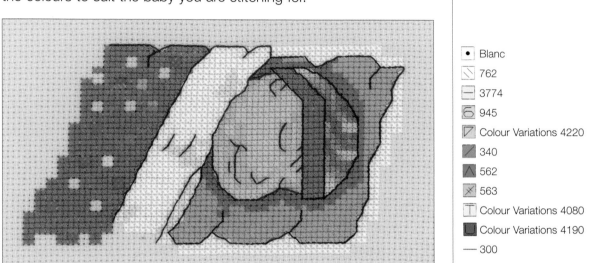

Sleeping baby

•	Blanc
⟍	762
—	3774
6	945
▱	Colour Variations 4220
▨	340
◢	562
⊠	563
⊤	Colour Variations 4080
▣	Colour Variations 4190
—	300

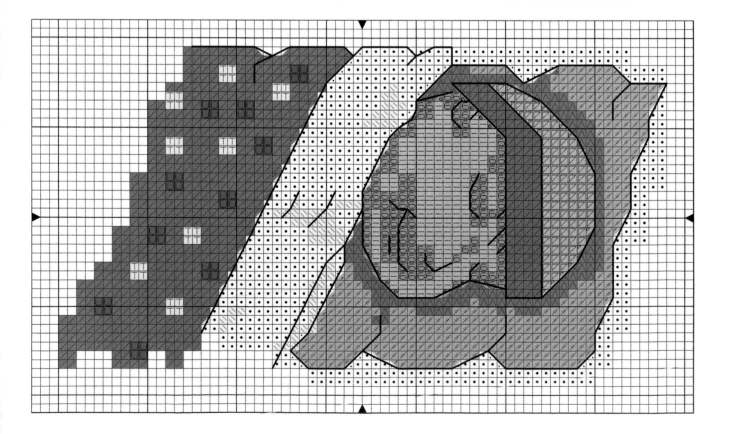

All toddlers enjoy a game of peek-a-boo. Try stitching this design onto the seat of a pair of dungarees, so it peeks out while you hold your child. It also makes a lovely card for grandparents and can be added to a baby book to celebrate first steps or crawling.

Peek-a-boo baby

•	Blanc
▓	799
−	3774
6	945
✕	563
◣	552
▷	973
◁	799 half cross stitch
—	300
●	300

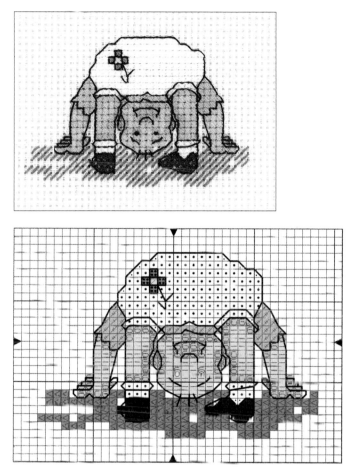

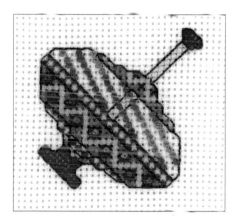

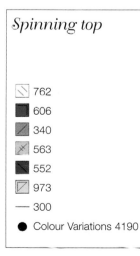

Spinning top

◺	762
■	606
◸	340
✕	563
◣	552
▱	973
—	300
●	Colour Variations 4190

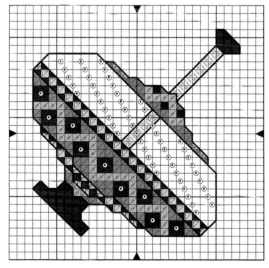

This simple spinning top design is bright, fun and versatile. It makes a great spot motif for bibs and bonnets, or add it as a patch to curtains (drapery) and bedding. The French knots are all worked using one colour variation and shade stitched in rows.

Feathered friends

*These assorted feathered buddies are great
motifs for those "difficult to stitch for" people.
Everyone's bound to have a favourite here.*

This pair of swans is ideal as an
anniversary keepsake card, or try
stitching it as a cover for your bird
watching notebook – just add wording
and/or a simple border for a lovely result.
If you are in a hurry, or if space is short,
stitch just one bird, either would look
good as a motif on a sampler.

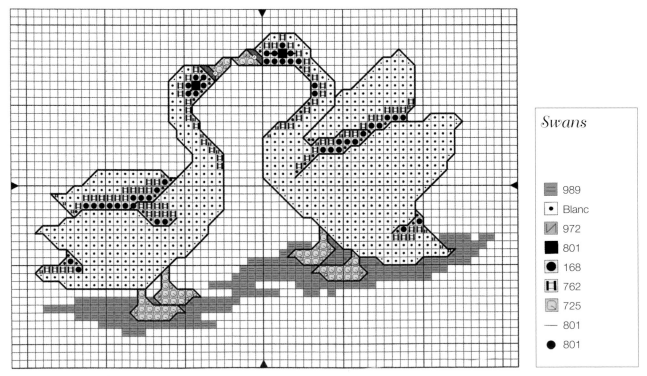

Swans

▤	989
⊡	Blanc
◹	972
■	801
●	168
⊞	762
▧	725
—	801
●	801

I love cockerels and the way they strut and pose (typical male behaviour!), particularly the ones with elaborate plumage, so I have tried to capture the vibrant gold and green shades here. This handsome chap would look great on country-style kitchen items, e.g. tea towels, pot holders and tea cosies. Why not try working just the head and neck ruff for an egg cozy?

Cockerel

⊞	561
⊞	562
◯	563
◆	801
⊞	780
✕	782
▢	783
⟋	3820
▼	738
⊟	3705
I	3706
⊥	Colour Variations 4070
—	801
●	Blanc

This bold, stencil-styled pair of brightly coloured parrots is one motif where you can throw away the thread key and use up any spare colours you've got in your workbasket. Stitch it as a picture for a summer house or onto conservatory cushions (pillows).

Parrots

- 793
- 740
- 553
- 604
- 792
- 321
- 3708
- 702
- 434
- 744
- 938

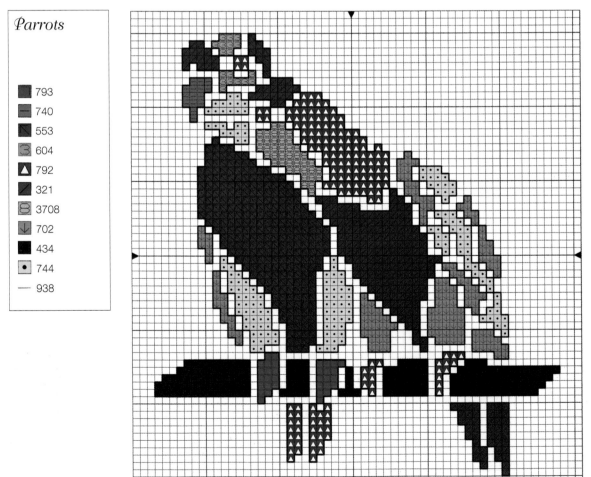

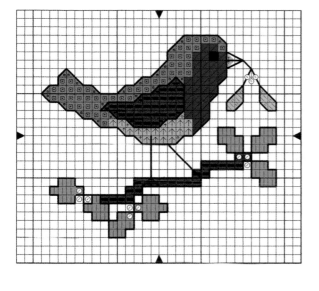

Robin

	704
	703
	321
	801
	729
	435
	739
–	703
—	801
●	321
●	746

French knots

Holly 321
Mistletoe 746

This cute little robin, with his bright red breast and mistletoe in his beak, is a real symbol of winter. Stitch it onto your birding rucksack, or as a quick, any purpose card. It also makes an ideal filler motif for a sampler, just omit the branch if space is limited.

This colourful motif forms a useful patch. Stitch it onto Aida fabric then back it with a piece of felt and appliqué it onto bags, rucksacks and even mp3 player cases. The flamingo on its own is a great motif for bath towels and flannels.

Flamingo

	793
△	792
✕	727
⦿	794
⊠	3832
	975
◹	726
—	938

The blue tit was probably the first bird I could recognize as a child, I just loved the blue shade so rarely seen in nature. This design makes up into an attractive any purpose card and is a good motif for a bird-themed sampler. Try stitching just his head onto the top of a bookmark.

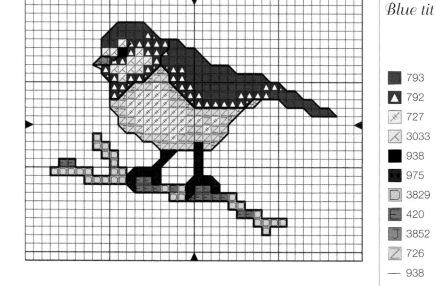

Blue tit

- ■ 793
- ▲ 792
- ✕ 727
- ◹ 3033
- ■ 938
- ■ 975
- ☐ 3829
- ☲ 420
- ⊔ 3852
- ◿ 726
- — 938

Duck

- ■ 793
- ⊗ 3708
- ↓ 702
- ✕ 727
- ◹ 3033
- ■ 938
- ■ 975
- ☐ 3829
- ⑤ 842
- — 702
- — 938

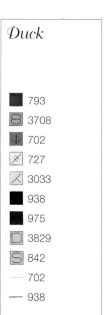

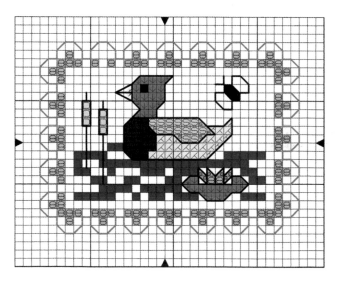

This stamp-style duck motif stitches up very quickly and you get a lot of results for very little effort. Stitch it onto hiking gear, e.g. rucksacks and hats, or use it as a motif for a bird watching notebook cover. It would also make a good little card for saying thank you, get well soon, or even just hello.

My only reason for including a puffin is that I just love them, they always seem to be "in on the joke", with a little half smile on their face. This is a great motif to add to bathroom towels and flannels, or to personalize your beach bag. It would also look brilliant on a mobile phone or compact disc carry case.

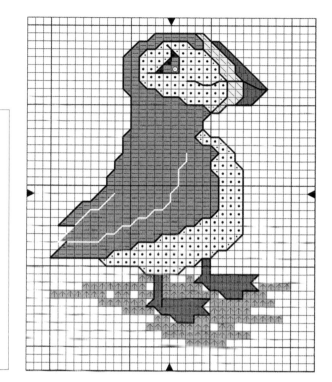

Puffin

1	741
–	310
•	blanc
◸	726
↥	422
✚	796
—	310
	Blanc
●	Blanc

I couldn't do a puffin and not include a toucan. The same cheeky face and a nonchalant air means this is a great motif for many purposes. It makes a great sampler motif, as it's a bird everyone recognizes, or stitch it onto a tie, if you know someone with the sartorial daring to wear it!

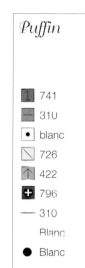

Toucan

◼	321
–	310
•	Blanc
◸	726
◩	972
◼	436
—	310
	Blanc

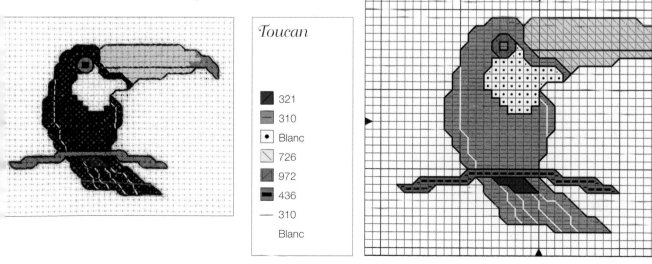

One of the most breathtaking sights in the bird world is a barn owl in full flight, illuminated by moonlight. Stitch this design on 11-count Aida to maximize its size and impact and turn it into a framed picture. Alternatively, try stitching just the owl onto a child's pencil case or a card.

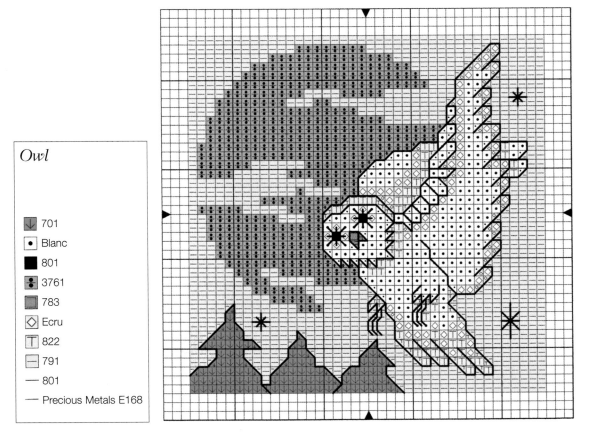

Owl

↓	701
•	Blanc
■	801
⬥	3761
▭	783
◇	Ecru
T	822
⊟	791
—	801
—	Precious Metals E168

Cats and dogs

Cats and dogs are always a popular subject matter
for stitchers, so whether you are a cat or a dog person
there is sure to be a motif to suit in this collection.

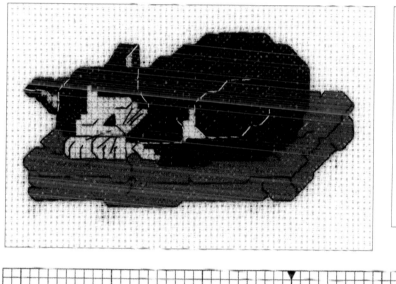

Sleepy cat

●	Blanc
◢	349
◩	817
△	310
△	225
-	310
	Blanc

Deceptively easy to
stitch, this sleepy cat
gives a pleasing result.
Use waste canvas, alter
the shades to match
your own cat and stitch
it onto his or her blanket.

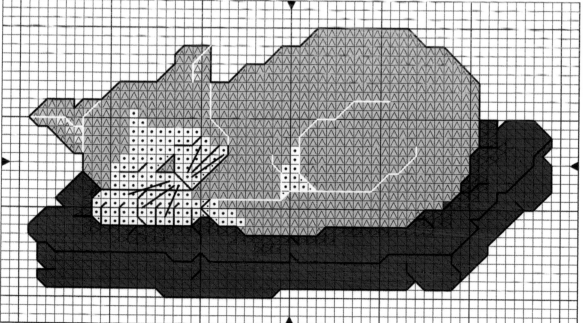

These delightful cats, sitting warm and snug on the window sill and silhouetted against the cold evening sky, are a good design for an anniversary card for a special couple. As it is a solid block of stitching it is also very suitable for stitching on waste canvas.

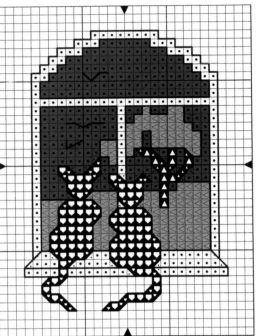

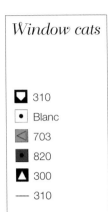

Window cats

◪	310
•	Blanc
◁	703
■	820
▲	300
—	310

Few can resist this cute trio of kittens, and it is also a very versatile motif. Stitch individual kittens scattered across an afghan, or use repeats of the trio to create a decorative border for bags and scrapbooks.

Cat trio

◆	801
•	Blanc
◁	703
■	793
•ǀ•	746
⊖	224
⊠	729
▪▪	680
▱	415
—	801

This sneaky cat, toying with a mouse, makes a cheeky little framed picture, or try stitching it onto a rucksack or bag. If you want a quick motif for a card, take a line down vertically through the center of the design and just stitch everything to the left, making sure you stagger the right edge slightly.

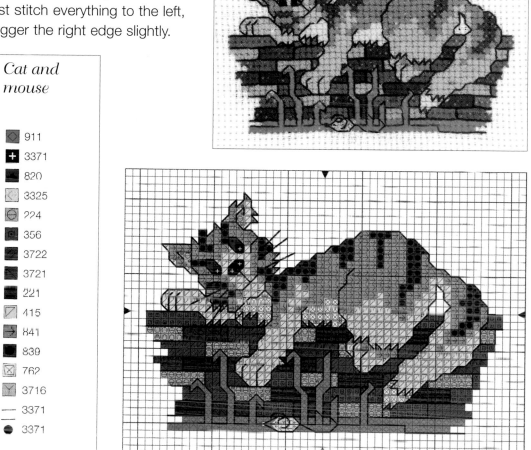

Cat and mouse

◇	911
✚	3371
◼	820
◪	3325
⊖	224
◪	356
◼	3722
◼	3721
◼	221
◿	415
➡	841
◼	839
⊠	762
Y	3716
—	3371
●	3371

This romantic pair of cats snuggling up together is perfect on a card for that someone special. Try stitching it onto the edge of a bed sheet or the corners of a pillowcase, altering the background shade to suit your décor.

Cat pair

�™	349
◼	820
V	3607
—	310

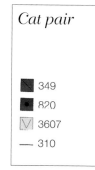

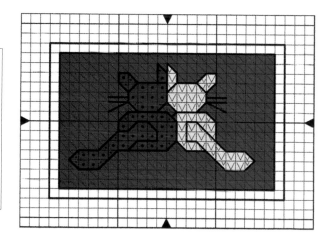

What better way to celebrate a new arrival in the family – be it a puppy or a baby! Stitch it onto blankets and baby items, or use it in a sampler to commemorate a birth or arrival. Change the border shade to blue for a baby boy, or a male puppy!

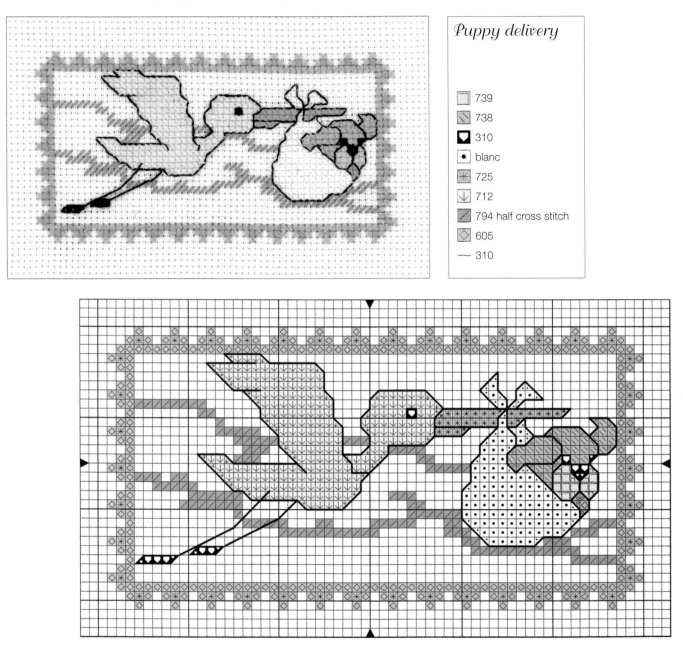

Puppy delivery

⬜	739
◺	738
◆	310
•	blanc
✳	725
↓	712
╱	794 half cross stitch
◇	605
—	310

Sick as a dog

☐ 739
◩ 738
Ɛ 437
▬ 436
▬ 435
• Blanc
✚ 3371
↓ 799
♡ 415
▮ 798 half cross stitch
▨ 3806
— 3371
● Blanc
● 3371

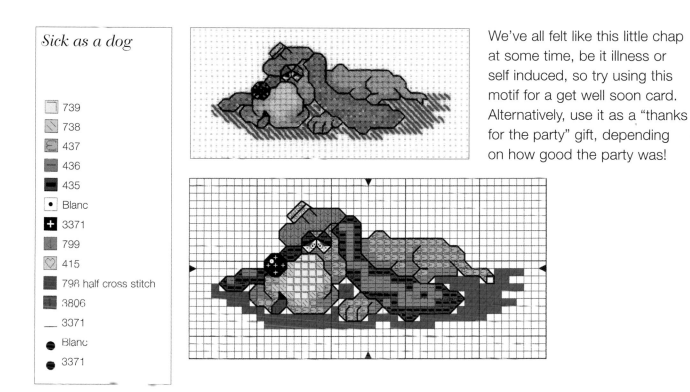

We've all felt like this little chap at some time, be it illness or self induced, so try using this motif for a get well soon card. Alternatively, use it as a "thanks for the party" gift, depending on how good the party was!

This happy fellow is about the cutest motif in the book. Try expanding the design by stitching more flowers or alter the bow colours to take advantage of spare threads from other projects.

Cute dog

▦ 208
• Blanc
✚ 3371
▮ 796
▮ 793
● 798
☐ 905
✳ 728
⊠ 3822
◵ 3823
▯ 3820
▪ 3829
▮ 3806
— 3371

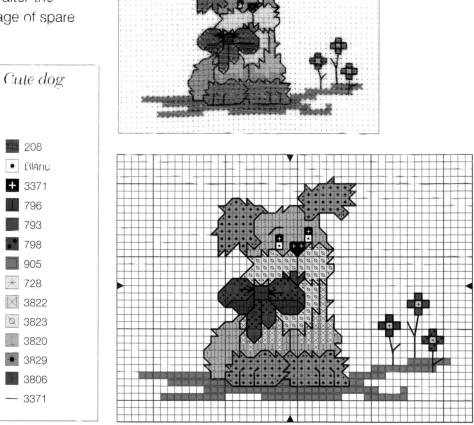

In my opinion there are few things more adorable in the dog world than a dalmatian puppy, this one reminds me of the one I had as a little girl. Stitch him as a picture for framing or onto a child's bag. He also makes a stylish addition to a dog or travel blanket, just use waste canvas.

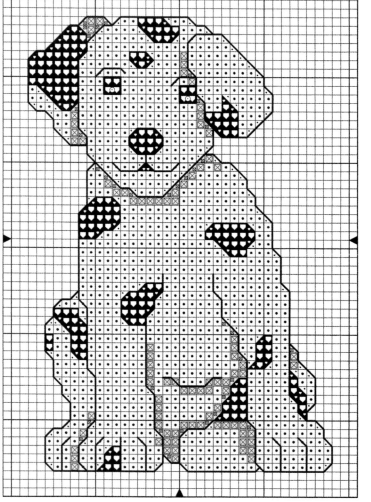

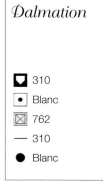

Dalmation

◨	310
•	Blanc
⊠	762
—	310
●	Blanc

This bleary party dog stitches up into a great party invite – he'll be loved by party animals both young and old. Suitable as a motif for a sampler, this design looks bright and cheery when also worked as a picture. For smaller spaces and projects try stitching just his head, party hat and trumpet.

Party dog

- ▨ 739
- ◩ 738
- ◪ 437
- ▨ 436
- ■ 435
- ▦ 208
- • blanc
- ◪ 798
- ▽ 799
- ▨ 905
- ✳ 728
- ▩ 208 half cross stitch
- ■ 3806
- ◣ 300
- — 3371
- — 905
- — 3806

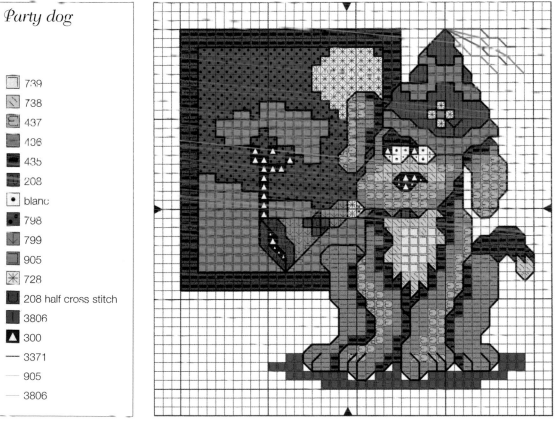

Borders

The quickest way to liven up large items is to add a bright border. They can be as simple or as complex as you like and they always create a pleasing result.

This house motif has a courtyard with a fountain, sun deck and an olive tree. It makes a perfect towel band on a "welcome to your new home" gift. Stitch an individual motif onto a sampler commemorating the move or add some wording such as "home sweet home".

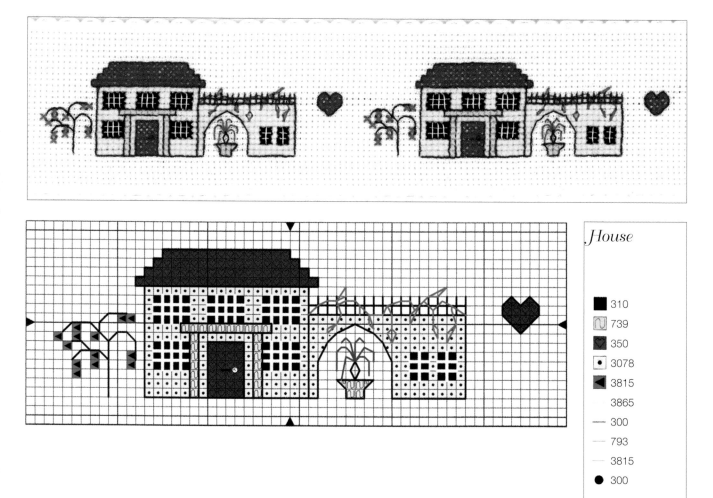

House

■	310
◪	739
◩	350
•	3078
◣	3815
	3865
—	300
—	793
—	3815
●	300

Everyone must remember playing
with those bright yellow rubber
ducks in the bath as a child. This
border can be stitched onto baby
towels or a toddler's bath robe.
Try stitching individual ducks
onto baby clothes or as a filler
motif on samplers.

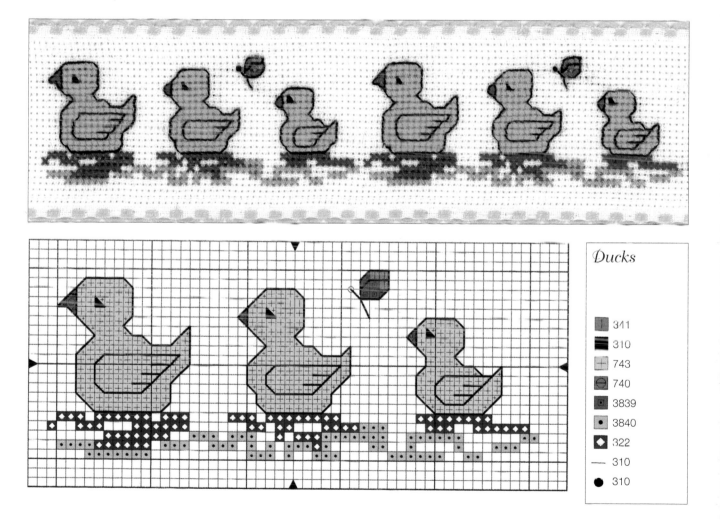

Ducks

▯	341
▬	310
✚	743
⊖	740
▣	3839
•	3840
◆	322
—	310
●	310

This decorative heart border is truly versatile. Add it to table
linens and towels or stitch it as a frame by simply rotating
the design through 90° for each side – the length will
depend on the picture you wish to frame. This motif
can also be used in scrapbooks or on samplers. For an
interesting twist, stitch the unstitched bits instead and
you'll end up with a row of hearts and single stitch borders.

Heart

⬛ 304

— 304

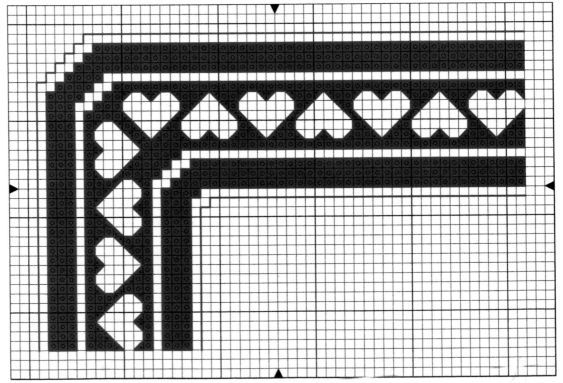

This silhouette border is good for adding to the lower edge of a roller blind (shade), brightening it up and forming a decorative piece whether the blind is completely rolled down or left partially up. Stitch as many repeats as required on a preformed band, commencing work at the center to ensure a balanced result.

Silhouette

■	310
▨	798
⊖	740
◈	797
✱	799
•	726
▢	743
◕	809
⌐	827
—	310

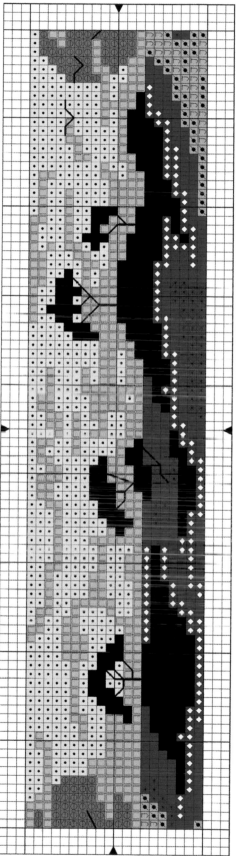

This stunning art deco design is suitable for larger scale projects. Try adding it to bedding or tableware, altering the shades to suit your décor. Use it as a frame for a large scale sampler, or stitch just the outer edge design if a more delicate border suits your project.

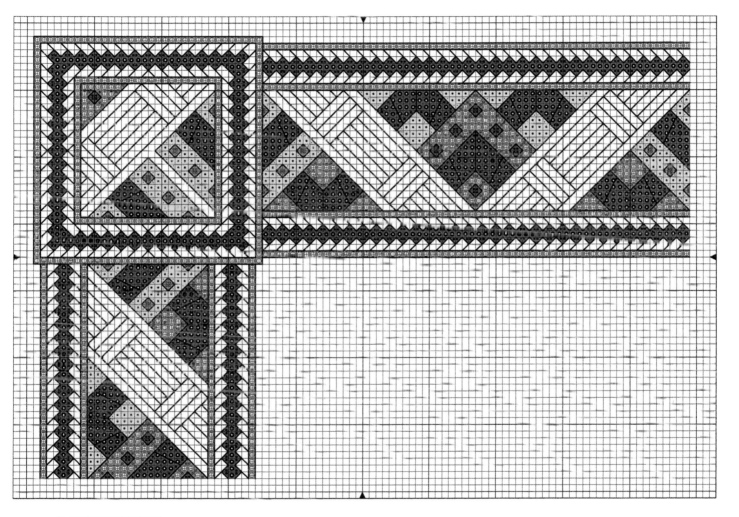

Art deco

- • 3689
- ⊕ 3688
- ◉ 3687
- — 902

This bold, bright border design is just as effective
when it is used as a single spot motif. Try adding
it to a bag or the edge of a pair of curtains (drapery),
changing the colour to suit your décor. Alternatively,
scatter the single floral motif across a patchwork
quilt, stitching them in different shades for impact.

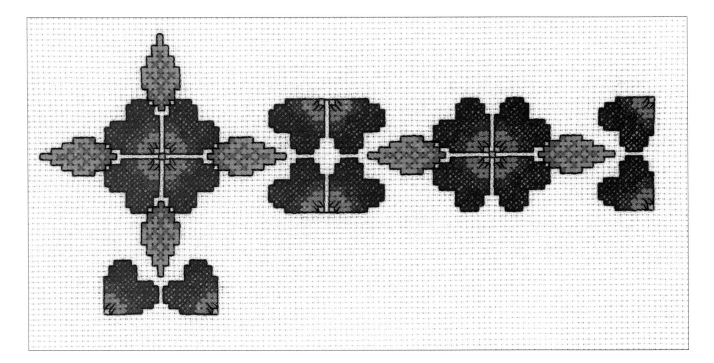

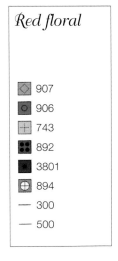

Red floral

◇ 907
◉ 906
╬ 743
▓ 892
■ 3801
⊕ 894
— 300
— 500

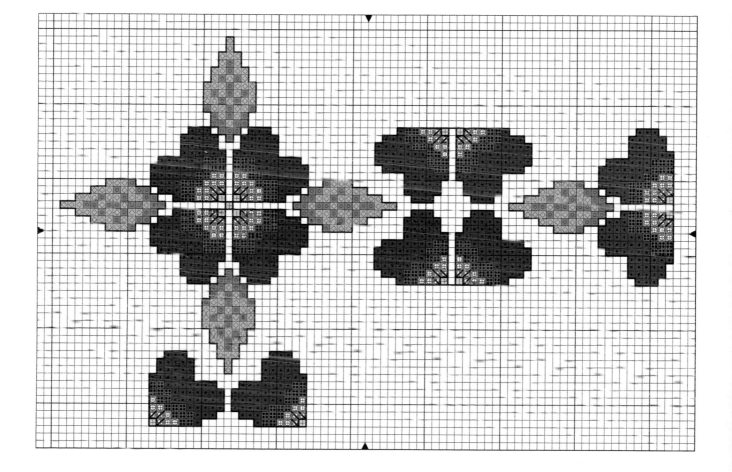

This striking mosaic-style border is a
great choice for bathroom projects.
Add it to towels and flannels or create
a border for a framed bathroom mirror,
making sure the final project is carefully
sealed against moisture penetration.

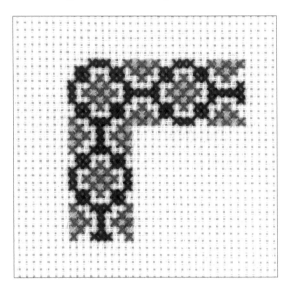

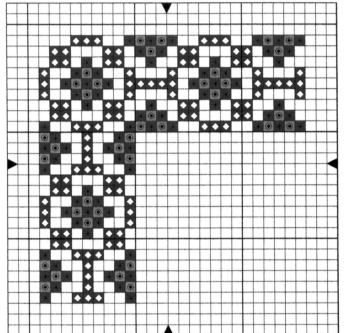

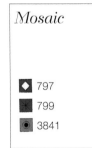

Mosaic

◆	797
✚	799
◉	3841

This silver and pastel bubble border stitches amazingly quickly, making it a good choice to cover large areas. It makes a great edging on bathrobes and gives a subtle lift to dull curtains (drapery), blinds (shades), sheets or table cloths.

Bubble

☐	3747
▨	Precious Metal Effects E168
●	818
⊞	967

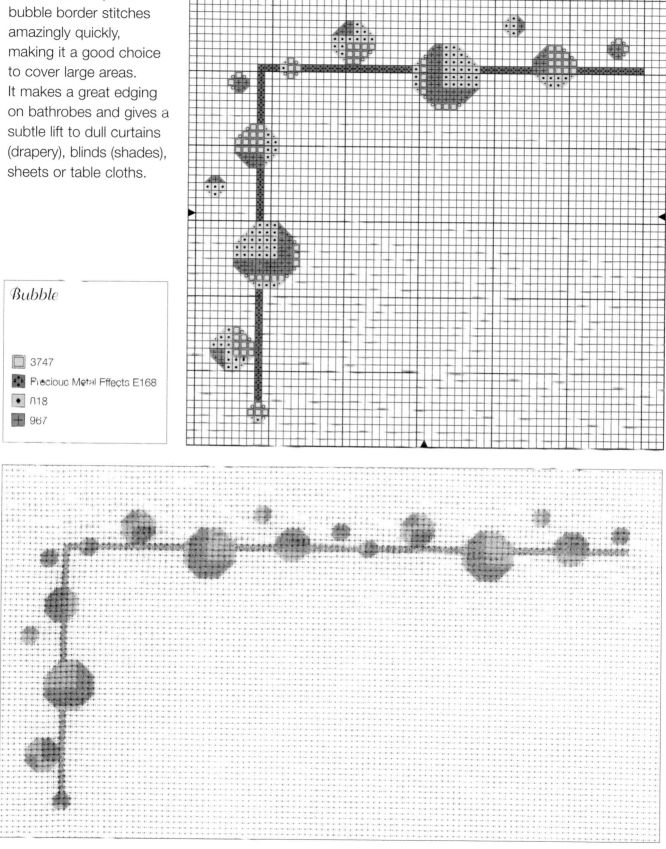

This bright rainbow bunny border is brilliant for jazzing up the nursery. Work it as a border onto curtains (drapery) and cot bumpers or stitch individual bunny and rainbow motifs scattered across a baby afghan (you can buy these specially made for cross stitch). This type of design is well suited to stitching with waste or plastic canvas as it contains no partial stitches.

Rainbow

▯	341
⊙	906
▬	3865
1	738
■	310
+	743
▮	798
◥	600
•	3801
▦	761
⊡	3839
•	3840
—	300

This delicate, blue, floral border stitches up very speedily. Work it as a picture frame on a sampler or add it to bedding and towels. Stitch individual flowers with a little bit of stem and a leaf for a quick spot motif on hankies and napkins.

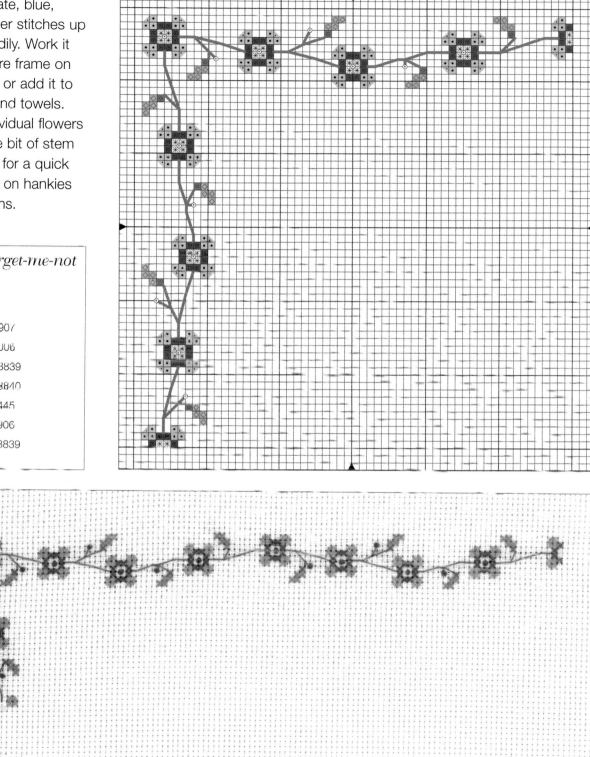

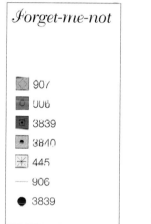

Forget-me-not

907
906
3839
3840
445
—	906
●	3839

Flowers

Flower designs are loved by all who cross stitch. They are versatile motifs that will grace any project small or large.

This stunning pasque flower has delicate foliage to balance out its bold, deep-coloured petals. It looks lovely on a pillowcase or nightdress bag and is ideal as a spot motif for a scrapbook or floral-themed sampler.

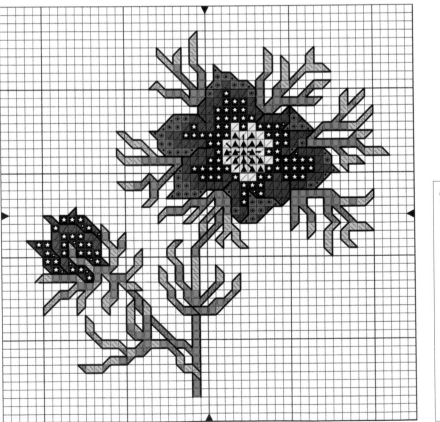

Pasque

◿	445
▲	444
◼	562
◥	563
★	3834
◼	3835
⦿	3836
—	500

The larger than life ox-eye daisy is a perfect sized motif when a quick card is needed. Use it as a corner motif on picnic napkins or scatter them over a table cloth. This design is also good for floral samplers or as a spot motif on a sofa throw.

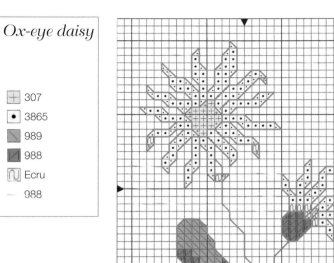

Ox-eye daisy

⊞	307
•	3865
◻	989
◼	988
ℕ	Ecru
—	988

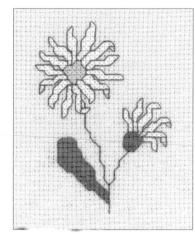

The blue and white theme is represented here with this subtle vase of forget-me-nots and hare bells. This makes a lovely picture for Mothers' Day or add lettering and a simple border to make a book cover.

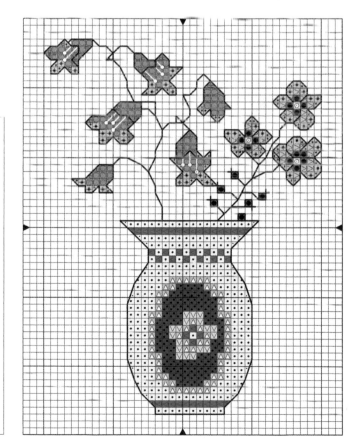

Blue floral

⧄	445
◼	792
•	3865
⬤	3839
◪	341
▷	3840
◼	340
∨	162
△	3755
◼	322
—	500
●	3865

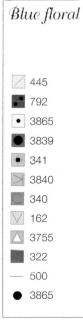

The ultimate symbol of romance is a single red rose bud. I've included this design because it looks fabulous stitched onto a corner of a pillowcase – as if it has been left by a fleeting visitor! You can also decorate cushion covers and afghans with this motif.

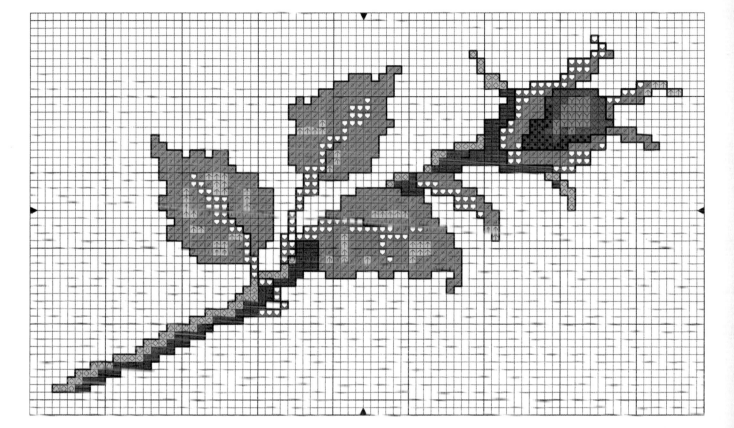

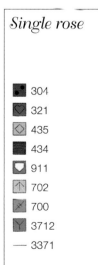

Single rose

■ 304
♥ 321
◇ 435
■ 434
▽ 911
↑ 702
✗ 700
Y 3712
— 3371

This quickly-stitched little cactus motif can be worked individually or repeated to form a border. Stitch it onto gardening items, such as a coverall apron, gauntlets or even a kneeling pad cover – for those of us whose knees aren't what they used to be!

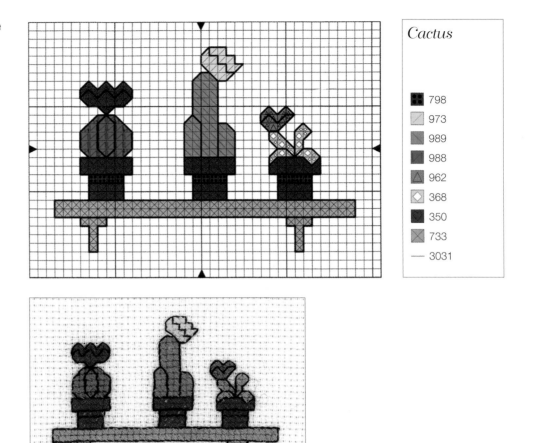

Cactus

▓	798
▨	973
◪	989
◼	988
△	962
◇	368
◙	350
✕	733
—	3031

This tiny buttercup motif is an instantly recognizable design. Stitch it on cards, gift tags or a bookmark. The small size makes it an ideal filler for a sampler or scrapbook.

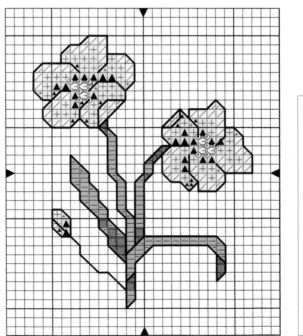

Buttercup

▨	445
✛	307
▲	444
▭	471
◼	470
▣	472
—	500
●	741

Ornamental poppies are bold and beautiful flowers and can be used to brighten up county kitchen-style items, such as tea towels, pot holders and apron pockets. Use individual flowers dotted across table cloths and in the corners of napkins.

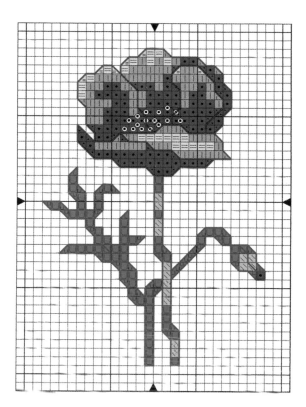

Ornamental poppy

■	498
▮	817
▤	666
▦	562
◪	563
—	561
●	3371

This hanging basket design, with a wrought iron bracket, is full of trailing lobelias and fuchsias. It is is suitable for a card for any occasion or as a filler motif for a sampler or scrapbook project.

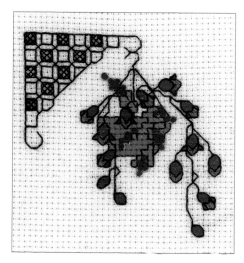

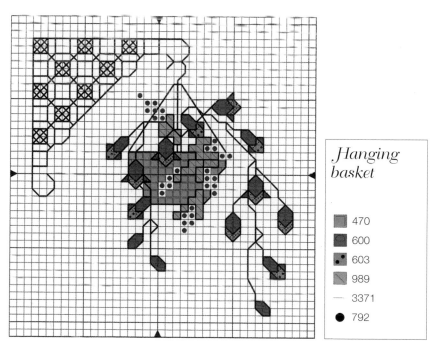

Hanging basket

▥	470
▦	600
⦁	603
◪	989
—	3371
●	792

A vivid trio of daffodils, planted in a terracotta pot, creates a lovely framed picture; you could also stitch a single flower onto a card or sampler. The watering can can be used on its own on garden seat cushions.

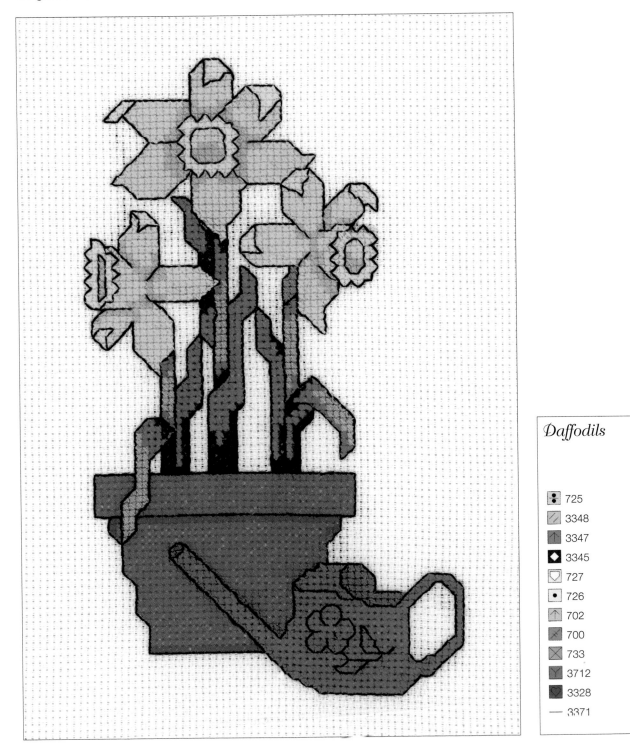

Daffodils

⋮	725
╱	3348
↑	3347
◆	3345
▽	727
•	726
↑	702
✗	700
✕	733
⅄	3712
♥	3328
—	3371

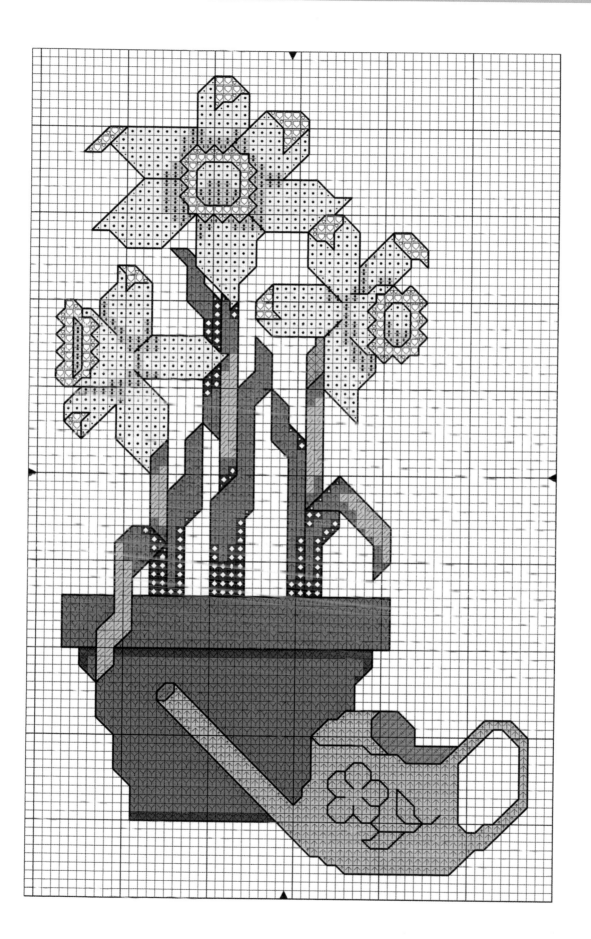

This medium sized, square floral motif is given a wonderful lift by the inclusion of colour variations thread in the design. It's perfect as a centerpiece for a dressing table cloth or side table cover. Try using it as a theme motif for a guest room by adding individual flowers to bedding, towels and face cloths.

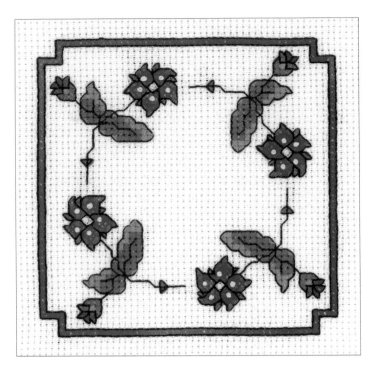

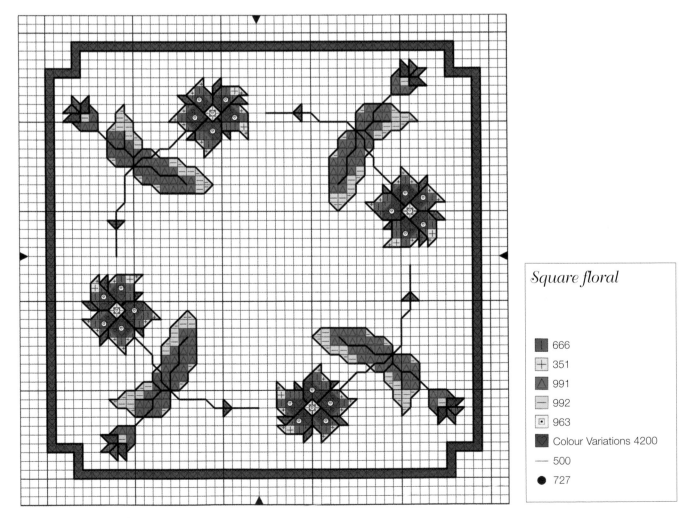

Square floral

▮	666
✛	351
◹	991
—	992
⊡	963
◼	Colour Variations 4200
—	500
●	727

Fun at the coast

Vivid coastal designs are a popular choice with stitchers everywhere. Children are particularly fond of the bright colours used in these motifs.

A stripy, bold beach ball, some fizzy pop and a bowl of ice cream, what more could you want on the beach? This design looks great stitched onto a beach bag or towel. Alternatively, break the design down into individual motifs and use them on a holiday sampler or stitched postcard.

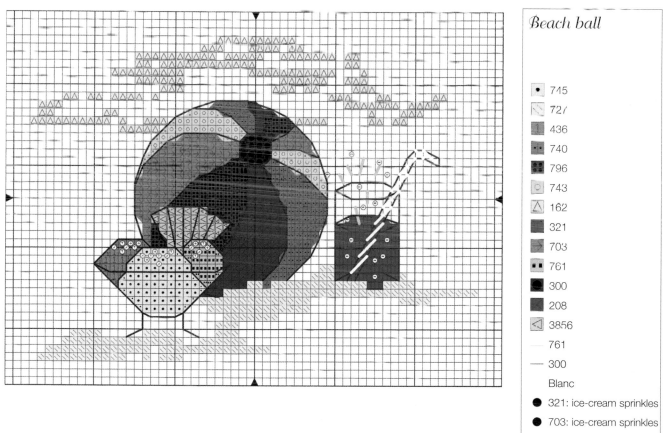

Beach ball

•	745
↖	727
1	436
∷	740
▦	796
○	743
△	162
■	321
↦	703
∷	761
■	300
■	208
◁	3856
—	761
—	300
	Blanc
●	321: ice-cream sprinkles
●	703: ice-cream sprinkles
●	761: fizzy drink
●	208: ice-cream sprinkles

This lighthouse is particularly effective when stitched as a birthday card for a little, and not so little, boy. It can also be stitched and then appliquéd onto a rucksack or mobile phone case. Try combining it with other motifs from this section for a fun, coastal-themed sampler.

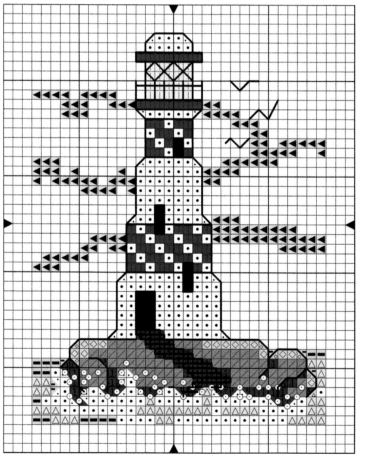

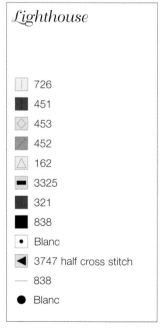

Lighthouse

⊥	726
■	451
◇	453
▨	452
△	162
▬	3325
■	321
■	838
•	Blanc
◀	3747 half cross stitch
—	838
●	Blanc

This crab design makes a cheerful card for any occasion. You can also add individual crab motifs to picnic items, such as a cloth, napkins and food covers. How about stitching one crawling out of your jeans pocket!

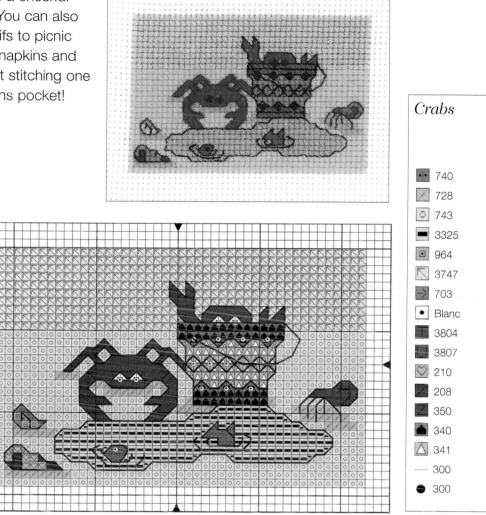

Crabs

- 740
- 728
- 743
- 3325
- 964
- 3747
- 703
- Blanc
- 3804
- 3807
- 210
- 208
- 350
- 340
- 341
- —— 300
- ● 300

What could be cooler than this smiling sun motif? Stitch it as a badge and add it to jeans and holiday bags. This design can also be used on an mp3 player, mobile phone or needle case, or to jazz up holiday scrapbook pages.

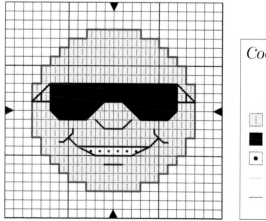

Cool sun

- 726
- 310
- Blanc
- —— 321
- —— 310

This under the sea trio of fish, coral and seaweed is great for brightening up a dull cloakroom. Try combining it with individual fish motifs stitched onto hand towels and facecloths. If you are after a larger design, try repeating it as a border for a bold edging.

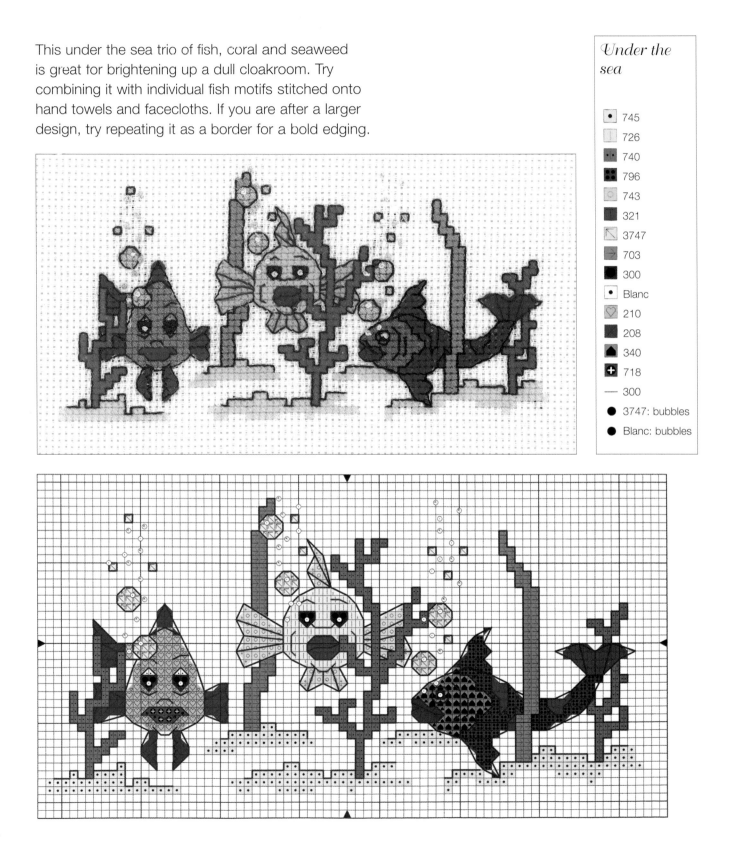

Under the sea

•	745
	726
	740
	796
	743
	321
	3747
→	703
	300
•	Blanc
♡	210
	208
▲	340
+	718
—	300
●	3747: bubbles
●	Blanc: bubbles

This cute single fish motif can be stitched in just an hour. Make it into a quick little card or work it into a bookmark for your holiday reading. This little guy also looks adorable on a child's flannel or bath robe.

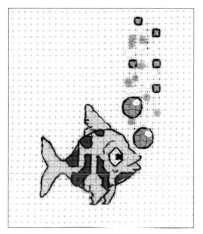

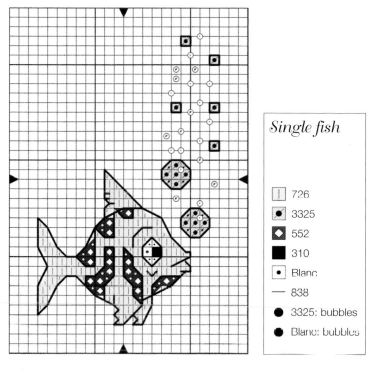

Single fish

▯	726
▣	3325
◆	552
■	310
▫	Blanc
—	838
●	3325: bubbles
●	Blanc: bubbles

I love the movement and action in this tiny motif. It makes an ideal card for the surfer dude in your family or stitch a whole group of surfers, in different wetsuits, to create a coastal scene. Try adding some crabs in the foreground to give an idea of distance.

Surfer

▯	726
▯	950
▣	740
▣	959
■	321
◆	552
▫	Blanc
—	838
●	Blanc

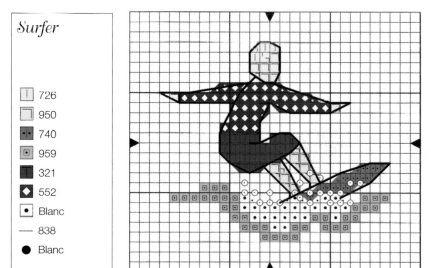

The perfect coastal image – a straightforward, no nonsense sail boat with the sea lapping around it. This makes a lovely framed piece for a seaside holiday home, or use it as a cover design for a stitched holiday scrapbook or photo album – go on, get those holiday snaps printed off the memory card for once!

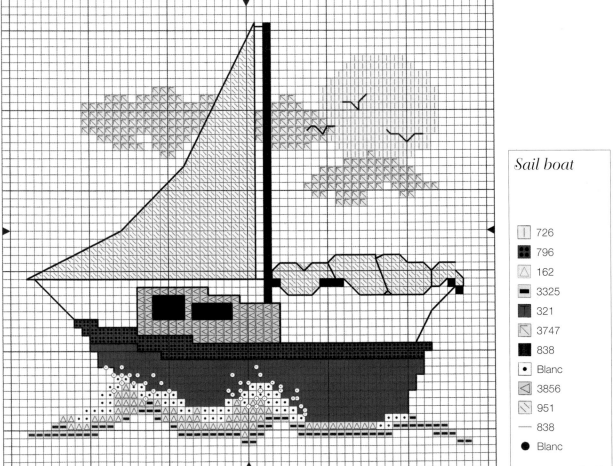

Sail boat

▯	726
▨	796
△	162
▬	3325
▮	321
◥	3747
■	838
•	Blanc
◁	3856
◳	951
—	838
●	Blanc

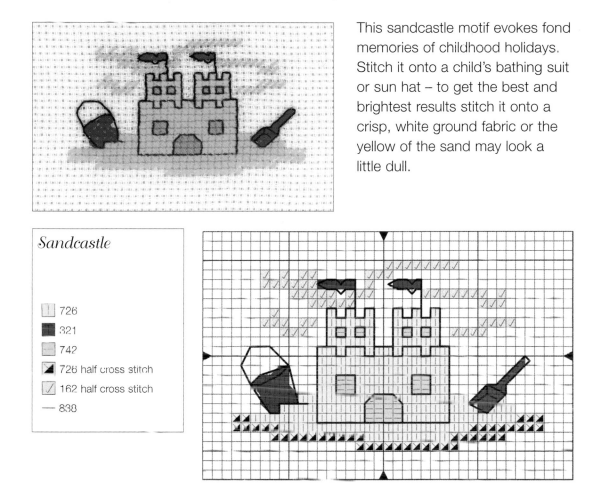

This sandcastle motif evokes fond memories of childhood holidays. Stitch it onto a child's bathing suit or sun hat – to get the best and brightest results stitch it onto a crisp, white ground fabric or the yellow of the sand may look a little dull.

Sandcastle

	726
	321
	742
	726 half cross stitch
	162 half cross stitch
—	838

This is another action packed motif, full of movement – you can almost see the windsurfer's muscles straining. Try adding it to a beach sampler, or combine it with the surf design on page 97 (they are both to the same scale) to make a larger coastal scene.

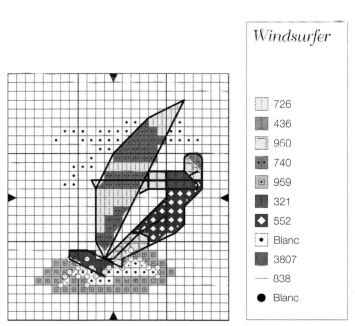

Windsurfer

	726
	436
	950
	740
	959
	321
	552
	Blanc
	3807
—	838
●	Blanc

Fantasy

I must confess this is a particularly indulgent section for me – I just love dragons, knights and fairytale castles, and I'm keeping my fingers crossed that you do too!

This shiny, metallic knight astride a bright white unicorn makes a stunning motif to start off this section. Stitch him as a little picture or add it to other motifs from this section to make a fantasy sampler. Try stitching your very own knight in shining armour phone case – go on I dare you to use it in public!

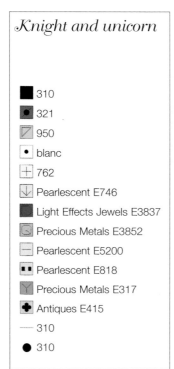

Knight and unicorn

- ■ 310
- ● 321
- ◪ 950
- • blanc
- + 762
- ↓ Pearlescent E746
- ■ Light Effects Jewels E3837
- ◩ Precious Metals E3852
- — Pearlescent E5200
- ▪▪ Pearlescent E818
- Y Precious Metals E317
- ✦ Antiques E415
- ---- 310
- ● 310

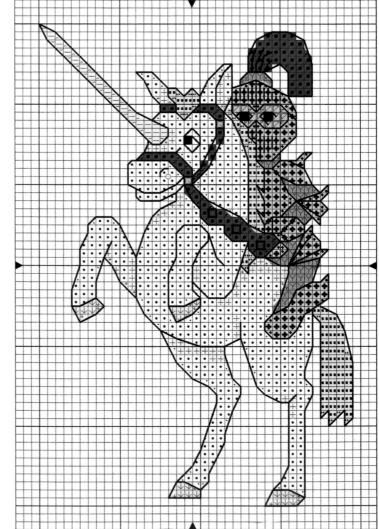

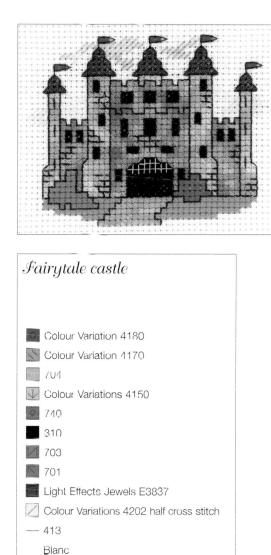

This fairytale castle is stitched using shades of colour variations thread, which makes every castle you stitch truly unique. Stitch it onto a child's bedding or a dressing gown pocket, or use it on an exercise book cover.

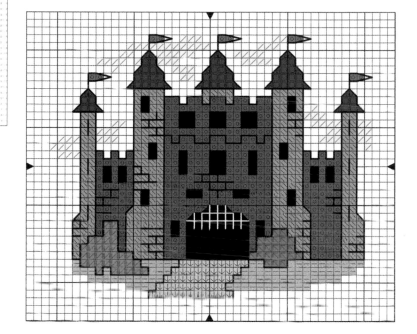

Fairytale castle

✿	Colour Variation 4180
◣	Colour Variation 4170
▨	704
↓	Colour Variations 4150
◉	740
■	310
◪	703
◥	701
▬	Light Effects Jewels E3837
◹	Colour Variations 4202 half cross stitch
—	413
	Blanc

This delicate little fairy is spreading a little of her magic to a frog. Use this design for a great "cheer-up" card for a friend, or stitch it onto a pair of bedroom curtains (drapery) to ensure a little magic in your child's dreams.

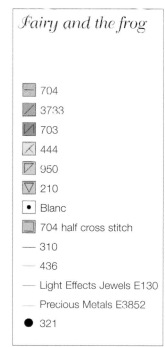

Fairy and the frog

⊟	704
◪	3733
◪	703
◿	444
◹	950
▽	210
•	Blanc
▢	704 half cross stitch
—	310
—	436
—	Light Effects Jewels E130
—	Precious Metals E3852
●	321

This bright trio of tournament tents conjures up images of the joust. Try combining it with other motifs from this section in a fantasy sampler – it's great for using up spare threads as the colours used on the tents aren't that important, as long as they don't clash too badly.

Tournament tents

▭ 966		◆ 971	
◨ 413		▢ 470	
◇ 955		▨ 704 half cross stitch	
⬊ 444		◹ 3688	
◤ 3746		▧ Rayon E30550	
♟ 333		◣ 553	
• 822		✚ 797	
▽ 210		— 413	
▢ 973			

Just to prove that not all dragons are fire breathing monsters this one is just as cute as can be. Stitch him as a picture, phone case or a card. He also looks great stitched onto baby items, such as a sleep suit or bib.

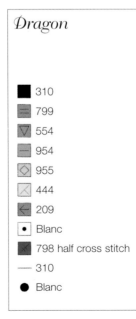

Ðragon

■	310
▤	799
▽	554
▤	954
◇	955
✕	444
←	209
•	Blanc
▨	798 half cross stitch
—	310
●	Blanc

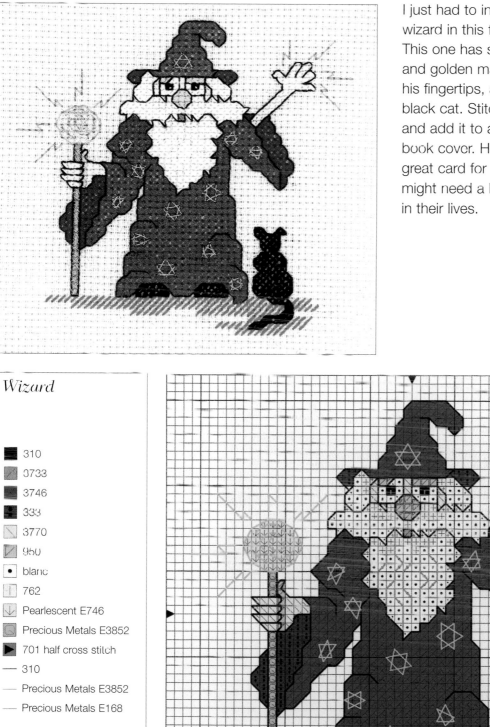

I just had to include a lovely old wizard in this fantasy collection. This one has silver in his beard and golden magic shooting from his fingertips, as well as a trusty black cat. Stitch him as a patch and add it to a schoolbag or book cover. He also makes a great card for anyone you think might need a little bit of magic in their lives.

Wizard

- ◼ 310
- ◪ 0733
- ◼ 3746
- ◼ 333
- ◹ 3770
- ◪ 950
- • blanc
- ⊡ 762
- ⬇ Pearlescent E746
- ◨ Precious Metals E3852
- ▶ 701 half cross stitch
- — 310
- — Precious Metals E3852
- — Precious Metals E168

This cheery little witch is an ideal motif for Halloween. Stitch her onto a table cloth and napkins or use it to liven up a Halloween costume. She also makes a fun invitation card – if you have the time!

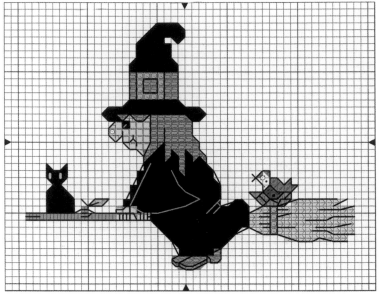

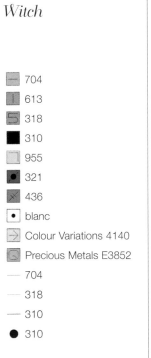

Witch

⊟	704
▮	613
⑤	318
■	310
☐	955
●	321
✕	436
•	blanc
→	Colour Variations 4140
▧	Precious Metals E3852
—	704
—	318
—	310
●	310

A spooky castle, some silky bats and a blood-red moon – yes it's Halloween! This motif can be stitched onto fabric and appliquéd anywhere you want it: clothing, party tableware, cards, etc.

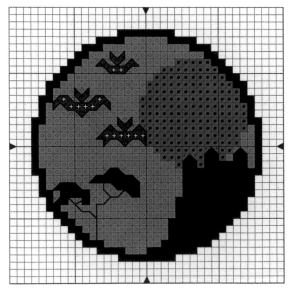

Bats

⊙	740
■	310
✚	Rayon 30310
●	321
—	310

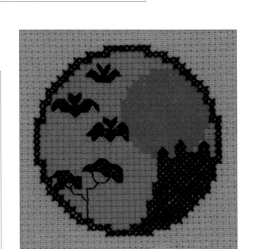

This pretty princess has gold in her bodice and the lace veil that trails from her hat. Stitch her for your little princess, adding it to curtains (drapery), bags and bedding. If time is pressing create a quick card by stitching everything above the horizontal halfway line.

Princess

■	Rayon 30606
▨	554
◩	3770
◪	950
⊕	3822
◙	746
▧	Precious Metals E3852
▦	704 half cross stitch
■	Rayon E30550
■	553
—	413
	Precious Metals E3852
●	Rayon 30606: jewels
●	413: eyes

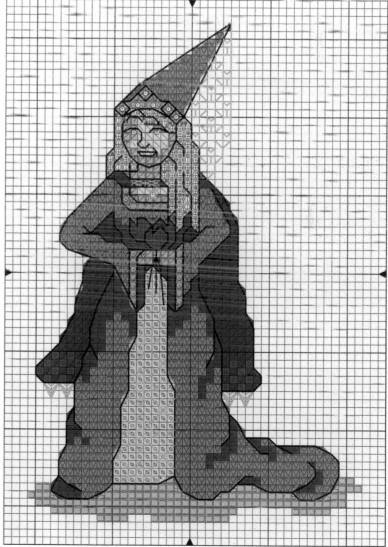

These two delightful fairies are floating in the air, with their hair trailing in the breeze. Stitch them individually onto a nightdress bag or sleepwear, or make your own ring of fairies wall hanging. Have fun choosing matching or contrasting thread for their outfits and wings.

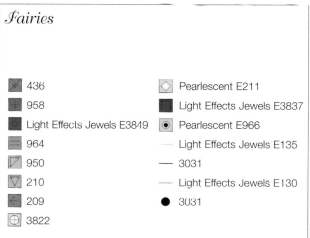

Fairies

✕ 436	◇ Pearlescent E211
✚ 958	◼ Light Effects Jewels E3837
◼ Light Effects Jewels E3849	⊙ Pearlescent E966
⊟ 964	— Light Effects Jewels E135
◿ 950	— 3031
▽ 210	— Light Effects Jewels E130
◧ 209	● 3031
⊕ 3822	

Keys

In the colour keys different symbols are used to denote the stitch required:
Solid block = cross stitch or half cross stitch
Single line = backstitch
Solid dot = French knot

Thread Conversion chart

This chart shows the Anchor equivalents of the standard DMC threads used in the book.

The speciality threads used can all be changed for any of the wide variety available. Kreinik threads are probably the most versatile, coming in a wide variety of thicknesses and finishes. Anchor also does an excellent metallic thread range called Reflecta. Many types of speciality threads can be obtained quite economically from internet auction sites.

Anchor	DMC
01	5200
002	White
006	353
008	3824
009	352
010	351
011	350
013	817
019	304
020	816
022	815
023	963
024	776
025	3716
026	894
027	893
028	956
029	891
031	3708
033	3706
035	3705
036	3326
038	956
039	309
040	956
041	893
042	309
043	815

Anchor	DMC
044	815
045	814
046	666
047	321
048	818
049	3689
050	957
052	899
054	956
055	604
057	601
059	3350
060	3688
062	603
063	602
065	3350
066	3688
068	3687
069	3803
070	3685
072	3865
073	963
074	605
075	3733
076	3687
077	3687
078	917
085	3609

Anchor	DMC
086	3608
087	3607
088	917
089	718
090	3836
092	553
094	917
095	3609
096	3608
097	554
098	553
099	552
100	327
101	550
102	550
103	211
108	210
109	209
110	208
111	208
112	3837
117	341
118	340
119	3840
120	3747
121	794
122	3807
123	791
127	823
128	3756
129	3325
130	799
131	798
132	797
133	796
134	820
136	799
137	798
139	797
140	3755
142	798
143	797
144	800
145	799
146	798
147	797
148	311
149	336
150	336
152	939
158	747

Anchor	DMC
159	827
160	827
161	813
162	517
164	824
167	598
168	807
169	806
170	3765
175	794
176	793
177	792
178	791
185	964
186	959
187	958
188	3812
189	991
203	954
204	913
205	911
206	564
208	563
209	912
210	562
211	918
212	561
213	504
214	368
215	320
216	562
217	367
218	319
225	702
226	702
227	701
228	700
229	910
230	909
231	453
232	452
233	451
234	762
235	414
236	3799
238	703
239	702
240	966
241	989
242	989
243	988

Anchor	DMC
244	987
245	987
246	986
253	472
254	472
255	907
256	906
257	905
258	904
259	772
260	3364
261	3053
262	3052
263	3362
264	3348
265	3348
266	471
267	469
268	937
269	936
271	819
273	645
274	928
275	746
276	543
277	830
278	3819
279	734
280	733
281	732
288	445
289	307
290	444
291	444
292	3078
293	727
295	726
297	973
298	972
300	745
301	744
302	743
303	742
304	741
305	725
306	3820
307	783
308	782
309	781
310	434
311	3827

313	977	387	Ecru	878	501	976	3752	1048	3776
314	741	388	842	879	500	977	334	1049	301
316	971	390	822	880	951	978	322	1050	3781
323	722	391	3033	881	945	979	312	1060	3811
324	721	392	642	882	758	1001	976	1062	598
326	720	393	3790	883	3064	1002	977	1064	597
328	3341	397	3024	884	920	1003	922	1066	3809
329	3340	398	415	885	739	1004	920	1068	3808
330	947	399	318	886	677	1005	816	1070	993
332	946	400	317	887	3046	1006	304	1072	992
333	900	401	413	888	3045	1007	3772	1074	3814
334	606	403	310	889	610	1008	3773	1076	991
335	606	410	995	890	729	1009	3770	1080	842
336	3341	433	996	891	676	1010	951	1082	841
337	3778	681	3051	892	225	1011	948	1084	840
338	3778	683	500	893	224	1012	754	1086	839
339	920	778	3774	894	224	1013	3778	1088	838
340	919	779	3768	895	223	1014	355	1089	3843
341	918	830	644	896	3721	1015	3777	1090	996
342	211	831	613	897	221	1016	3727	1092	964
343	3752	832	612	898	611	1017	316	1094	605
347	3364	842	3013	899	3782	1018	3726	1096	3753
349	301	843	3012	900	648	1019	315	1098	3801
351	400	844	3012	901	680	1020	3713	1200	62
352	300	845	730	903	3032	1021	761	1201	48
355	975	846	3011	905	3021	1022	760	1202	112
357	433	847	3072	906	829	1023	3712	1203	57
358	433	848	927	907	832	1024	3328	1204	107
359	801	849	927	914	407	1025	347	1206	115
360	898	850	926	920	932	1026	225	1207	99
361	738	851	924	921	931	1027	3722	1208	95
362	437	852	3047	922	930	1028	3685	1209	126
363	977	853	372	923	699	1029	915	1210	121
365	435	854	371	924	731	1030	3746	1211	93
366	951	855	370	926	712	1031	3753	1212	67
367	738	856	370	928	3761	1032	3752	1213	101
368	437	858	524	933	543	1033	932	1214	125
369	402	859	523	936	632	1034	931	1215	114
370	434	860	522	939	3755	1035	930	1216	94
371	975	861	935	940	824	1036	3750	1217	104
372	738	862	520	941	792	1037	3756	1218	105
373	3828	868	3779	942	738	1038	519	1219	108
374	420	869	3743	943	422	1039	518	1220	51
375	869	870	3042	944	869	1040	647	1223	53
376	3776	871	3041	945	834	1041	844	1243	111
378	841	872	3740	956	613	1042	504	4146	950
379	840	873	3740	968	778	1043	369	5975	3830
380	838	874	834	969	223	1044	895	8581	3022
381	938	875	3817	970	3687	1045	436	9046	321
382	3371	876	3816	972	3803	1046	435	9159	828
386	3823	877	3815	975	828	1047	402	9575	758

Index